HOCKEY FOR BEGINNERS

HOCKEY
FOR BEGINNERS

BY KEVIN WALSH

FOUR WINDS PRESS·NEW YORK

LIBRARY OF CONGRESS CATALOGING IN PUBLICATION DATA

Walsh, Kevin.
    Hockey for beginners.

    Includes index.
    SUMMARY: Text, photographs, and diagrams introduce
the fundamentals of ice hockey.
    1. Hockey—Juvenile literature.   [1. Hockey]
I. Title.
GV847.25.W34   796.9′62   76–17528
ISBN 0–590–07379–6

Published by Four Winds Press
A Division of Scholastic Magazines, Inc., New York, N.Y.
Copyright © 1976 by Kevin Walsh
All rights reserved
Printed in the United States of America
Library of Congress Catalog Card Number: 76–17528
1   2   3   4   5   80   79   78   77   76

CONTENTS

INTRODUCTION

There isn't a faster or more exciting game than ice hockey. It's a combination of speed, strength and pure guts that makes it a fun game to play and watch.

The game can be traced back to Europe where a form of field hockey was played many hundreds of years ago with a ball and sticks. In North America a game was played with curved sticks and a ball on frozen turf, and this too was a form of hockey, and the precursor of the game we discuss in detail in this book—ice hockey.

But some historians believe that a form of ice hockey was played in European countries long before the game was played here in North America. But it is pretty well established that the first organized hockey was played in Montreal, Halifax and Kingston, Canada during the middle 1800s.

It's reported by historians of the game that soldiers in Kingston, Ontario strapped skate blades to their boots, and used field hockey sticks to hit the ball around in games played on the St. Lawrence River.

The enthusiasm for this game played by the soldiers quickly spread across Canada and down into the United States. By the turn of the century there was a national hockey championship being played in Canada for a challenge cup called the Stanley Cup.

Soon after, the game of ice hockey became a professional sport in Canada with the organization of the National Hockey League. The game spread into the States in cities like Boston, New York, Detroit and Chicago.

In 1967 the NHL expanded from a six-team league to 12 teams and before long added more cities as hockey became the fastest growing professional sport. By the early 1970s still another league was formed for professional players, the World Hockey Association, and this league also made an impact on the game of hockey.

The spectacle of hockey as played professionally is unlimited. There has been an influx of European born and developed players in recent years with the arrival of the WHA and they too have improved the game by their great skating and stick-handling capabilities.

Hockey is a popular game because every boy is given an equal opportunity to play the game. Unlike some other sports, size is not the prime requisite for playing the game. The basic ingredient of a hockey player is dedication, mastery of the fundamentals, constant practice and the desire to play the game to the best of your ability.

KEY TO FIGURES

⟶	SKATING DIRECTION
∿∿∿⟶	SKATING WITH PUCK
− − − ⟶	PASS
C, LW, RW LD, RD	YOUR TEAM
Ⓖ, LW, RW, LD, RD	OPPONENTS' TEAM
CW	CHECKING WING
Ⓒ	PLAYER IN POSSESSION OF PUCK
DW	DEFENSIVE WING
FC	FORECHECKER
P K	PENALTY KILLER

HOCKEY FOR BEGINNERS

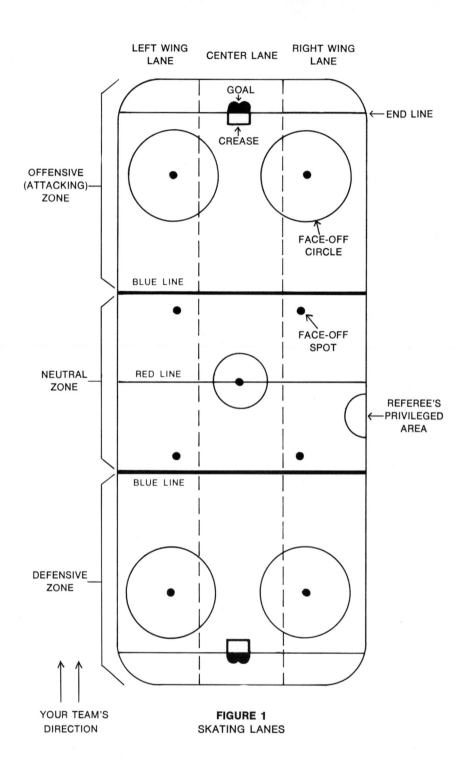

LEFT WING LANE   CENTER LANE   RIGHT WING LANE

GOAL

CREASE

← END LINE

OFFENSIVE (ATTACKING) ZONE

FACE-OFF CIRCLE

BLUE LINE

NEUTRAL ZONE

RED LINE

FACE-OFF SPOT

← REFEREE'S PRIVILEGED AREA

BLUE LINE

DEFENSIVE ZONE

YOUR TEAM'S DIRECTION

FIGURE 1
SKATING LANES

PLAYING POSITION

When you step onto the ice, you should know the layout of the rink or skating surface. You should know where you are going and what you should be doing every minute you're on the ice.

Let's start by dividing the rink into three parts. The area from the net your goaltender is guarding to the nearest blue line is called your team's *defensive zone*. From blue line to blue line (this includes the red line) is the *neutral zone*, and the section from the far blue line to the opponent's goal is the offensive or attacking zone (see Figure 1).

As you learn the basics of the game, you'll soon find out that there is a different responsibility attached to playing your position depending on whether the puck is in the defensive, neutral, or offensive zone, and depending on who has the puck.

A hockey team is made up of: a forward line composed of a center and two wings, whose primary job is to score; a left defenseman and a right defenseman, whose primary job is to prevent the opposition from getting a good shot at the net; and a goaltender, whose responsibility is to keep the puck out of the team's net.

With six players on the ice striving to score a goal while preventing the opposition from scoring, every individual must know the fundamentals of positional play. As a left winger or right defenseman, you have certain responsibilities depending on the situation.

If your team has the puck, you must concentrate on offense. If the opposition has possession of the puck, your thoughts must immediately turn to the defensive side of the game.

It really is a matter of teamwork. A wing who is skating back toward his goal to help out his defensemen and goaltender and trying to regain the puck from the other team is as important to the overall defensive play of a team as the goaltender. He is called a backchecking wing. Everyone on the ice has particular areas of responsibility.

It is very important that you learn your position well and stay within your areas of your responsibility during the game. It's helpful to learn everyone's job so that you have a better understanding of who should be doing what at all times. But the most important thing is that you get your job done.

Three imaginary lanes divide the rink into equal parts (see figure 1). For example, the right wing should operate in the third of the ice from the boards to an area 25 to 30 feet in from the boards. He should go up and down that lane, forechecking and backchecking. If the situation requires it, he can skate over into the center's lane, but he should rarely be found in the far lane. That belongs to the left winger.

Young hockey players have a habit of chasing the puck wherever it goes. This is something you'll have to strive to overcome. Chasing the puck breaks down the theory of positional play. If you have the puck in your lane and you notice two or three opposing players on your side of the ice coming at the puck, take a look around. If the opposition is chasing the puck all over the ice, their position play has broken down, and you should be able to pass the puck to an unguarded teammate, who should have a clear path to the opposing team's net.

INDIVIDUAL PREPARATION

On the day of a game your physical and mental preparations should start several hours before face-off.

Professional players generally have a planned schedule on the day of a game. They have definite eating habits. Most will eat a steak four or five hours before the game and then not eat again until after the game.

Some athletes will vary their diet. But, generally, professional athletes follow a well-balanced diet that is heavy in protein.

You, too, must give some thought to your eating habits. You shouldn't show up for a game with a stuffed feeling. It will affect your play. In fact some coaches feel that a younger player shouldn't eat much before a game.

The same holds true for practice. You won't get good results if you aren't ready for work. So if you have to eat before playing, try to eat easily digestible foods like meat, cheese or eggs. Limit your intake of milk or carbonated beverages to a 10-ounce glass.

The mental side of hockey requires special attention, too. This is why professional players normally take a nap late in the day. It accomplishes a couple of important things. You should be rested when you play a game. The set pattern of living is designed to enable him to think about hockey, and nothing else, on the day of the game. Distractions that might tire a player or take his mind off the game at hand are to be avoided. For this reason, some teams will take the players to a suburban hideaway during the playoffs.

A nap serves as a relaxer for your body and, at the same time, starts the mental process of thinking about the opponent you are going to face. A good hockey player has a "book"—a knowledge of a player or a team's strength and weakness—on the opposition. If he's a goaltender he'll be thinking about the dangerous scorer. The defenseman has to think about the good-skating forward and what his tendencies are in particular situations; while the centers and wings are thinking about their own game plans. Does the opposing goaltender have a weakness for high shots or low shots? In the line match-ups, who will be my check? What does he like to do?

There are exceptions to every rule. The great defenseman, Bobby Orr, arrives at the rink three or four hours before the start of a game. He blocks out everything but the game at hand from his mind, and lets the game build up inside of him so that when it's time to drop the puck he's ready to play hockey.

Bobby Hull is just the opposite. He'll arrive an hour before the game, with his million-dollar smile, and sign autographs for every kid in sight. Hull doesn't get himself all psyched up. He just seems to turn on a switch when the word is given to head out to the ice for the game. Once the puck drops, Hull plays as if he had been sitting in an isolation booth for eight hours thinking about nothing but the game.

A young player should fall somewhere between Orr and Hull. It's not necessary to arrive at the rink three or four hours early, and yet it's not a good idea to wait until the final minute before getting mentally prepared.

You should arrive in your team's dressing room in plenty of time to tape and prepare your sticks. Always have a standby ready in case you break a stick. And always allow yourself enough time to put your equipment on without rushing.

It never fails to happen that the player who comes rushing in at the last minute and is hurrying to get dressed will break a skate lace —and all of a sudden he's in a panic.

4

Such a panic situation is a distraction that takes away from the mental preparation you should normally be going through as you dress for the game.

The coach has prepared a game plan in most instances. It has been worked on in practice. Now it's time to put the plan to work. Think about how the other team likes to come out of its own end. How are you going to forecheck? If you have any questions, now is the time to ask them.

EQUIPMENT

Special care should be taken with your equipment. Although it is expensive, it will last a long time if precautions are taken when storing it after a game.

Your age and size should determine the type of equipment you wear. It doesn't make sense for a player under twelve to be wearing a pro-line pair of shin pads, gloves, or elbow pads. The equipment is usually too big and heavy for a boy this age and really hurts him more than it helps him. Start with properly fitting equipment.

The equipment is designed to provide you with protection while you are playing the game. It's something you should never be without.

Most teams will require a player to wear a helmet, mouthpiece, shin pads, shoulder pads, gloves, elbow pads and a protective cup. Hockey pants have a special protective padding that completes the job of properly outfitting a player. A complete uniform is best.

There are individuals who discard certain pieces of equipment because they feel that it's uncomfortable and gets in the way. This is not the proper attitude. Sometimes a pair of elbow pads, for example, may take a little while to break in. But you must live with this slight inconvenience in the beginning. The equipment, when properly fitted and broken in, is designed to prevent injury.

Forget that elbow pad and you'll risk chipping an elbow, which could be a costly lesson. Bone chips in the elbow often require surgery and could force you out of the lineup for several weeks, if not for the entire season. In comparison, that little stiffness you will feel when you try to flex your arm with new equipment doesn't seem that bad, does it? It's a great deal easier to wear it than to try to rebuild a limb to its original size and strength after surgery.

By proper fit I mean equipment that is comfortable once it has been worn a few times and broken in. It should not be too loose and definitely not so tight that it will interfere with blood circulation.

Skating is the most important part of the game, therefore it follows that the skates you buy are the most important part of your personal equipment.

Youngsters who have trouble learning to skate are often said to have weak ankles. Generally speaking, "weak ankles" are the result of the wrong skate size or skates that haven't been tightened properly.

The correct fit is a must. It will make you a better skater. Many parents feel that they should buy a pair of skates a size too large so that a youngster can get a couple of seasons' wear out of them. The typical solution to the problem of improper fit is that parents will tell the young hockey player to put on an extra pair of socks. Extra socks are not the answer to getting a correct fit.

Get a pair of skates that are the same size as your street-shoe size. Most professionals wear skates that are a size to a size-and-a-half smaller than their shoe size. They want a tight-fitting boot. But I don't recommend this to a boy with growing feet.

A skate that is a good fit will give you plenty of support. Pull your laces tight, but not so tight that they interfere with the circulation in your feet. I think you'll find that very few skaters with properly fitting skates will develop a case of "weak ankles." If added support is needed, pick up a pair of hockey-style ankle wraps. These are made of a stiff foam rubber material and wrap around the ankle from one side of the foot to the other (not completely around). Ankle wraps will give a little added support to a beginner.

The shin pad is an important item. Forwards will need shin pads that are light. If they are heavy, they slow you down and affect your skating speed. The defenseman, on the other hand, needs a little heavier pad that offers added protection because he uses his legs to block shots and the pad must absorb the impact.

Be sure that your shin pad gives protection to your knee. Many professionals line the inside of their pads with cotton for added protection, especially in the knee area.

Shoulder pads have a fiberglass cap to cover the shoulder and the upper arm area. I won't emphasize again the value of elbow pads, but don't forget the gloves that are designed to protect your hands.

Hockey pants should fit properly so they will provide you with protection in the hip, thigh, and rib areas. The pants should hang just above your knee. If pants are too big or too small, they'll restrict your skating and also reduce the amount of protection they give.

It's important that you wear a protective cup. They are sold in all sporting goods stores. The cup with a rubber lining is inserted into a specially designed athletic supporter with a pouch.

There are two pieces of equipment that have been shunned by professional hockey players in the National Hockey League (NHL) and the World Hockey Association (WHA)—helmets and mouthpieces. I've noticed that more young players coming out of the junior hockey ranks are now wearing helmets. It may be a trend.

The stars of the game, such as Orr, Phil Esposito, Gordie Howe, Hull, and Brad Park, never bothered to use this important piece of equipment. But Gordie Howe's two sons, Mark and Marty, who jumped from the Toronto Marlies in the Ontario Hockey Association to the WHA, continued to wear the helmets they grew accustomed to while playing junior hockey. The same is true of Dennis Potvin, who was paid several thousand dollars to sign a pro contract with the New York Islanders.

With the stars of the future such as the Howes and Potvin wearing helmets, I feel others at the professional level will follow their example. When this happens, it will be easier for a young hockey player to accept the fact that he must have a helmet on at all times. It is for his own protection.

A good helmet gives you protection at the back of your head, in the temple and forehead areas, and on the top of your head. As of January 1, 1974, the Canadian Standards Association (CSA) established safety regulations for hockey helmets sold in that country. These require that each helmet have a layer of foam padding three-quarters of an inch thick in a shell of fiberglass or heavy plastic. I prefer a suspension-type helmet, in which the head is not in contact with the outer shell. I feel that it offers the best protection. And when you have your helmet on, be sure it's secured.

There are many different styles of mouthpieces. Some go outside the mouth (figure 2) and others are worn inside. The inside mouthpiece offers the best protection. This can be made by your own dentist. It really isn't too expensive and allows you to talk and breathe normally. Like some of the other equipment you use, it takes a little time to get accustomed to.

Another important part of your equipment is the stick you use. Do you know if you are a left-hand or a right-hand shot? The hand that you place lower on the shaft of the stick is the hand that determines what kind of shooter you are.

It's best for a beginning hockey player to get a straight-bladed stick. It allows you to develop your puck-handling skills. If you must bow to the times, get a stick with just a slight curve in the blade.

Most sticks on the rack in the store are too long for a young hockey player, and will have to be cut down to size. As a rule of thumb, the stick should be long enough to reach the player's chin (figure 3) when he is standing with his skates on.

Another consideration in choosing a stick is what lie is best for you. The lie is the angle of the stick to the ice, and for forwards and defensemen ranges from four to seven. The proper lie is determined by what feels comfortable to the player. If you're a straight-up skater who carries the puck close to your body, you'll find a six or a seven lie most comfortable. If you crouch a little, bend your body slightly, and carry the puck well out in front, a four or five lie would be proper. If you are confused by this point, take a lie five stick, and as your game develops, you can see what is best suited to the way you play.

Your equipment should be aired and dried after every use. Don't leave it rolled up in a ball in your equipment bag. And be certain to wipe the blades of your skates dry after you are finished using them so they won't rust.

The skates should receive special care. Professional hockey players have their skates sharpened for every game, and some for every practice as well. You will know that your skates need to be sharp-

FIGURE 2. A mouthguard should be part of your equipment. Be certain it is attached properly. Now you are properly protected.

FIGURE 3. Your stick should be long enough to reach your nose when you are standing on skates. Don't have a stick that is too long.

ened when you feel them slipping from under you as you attempt to turn. This means you have lost your edge. A dull skate blade can be responsible for injuries, so be sure to have your skates sharpened at all times. To prevent dulling, be sure you don't walk on cement or similar-type surface or come in contact with metal.

The goaltender has specialized equipment. His skates have a different blade and an added protective covering on the boot.

His gloves are different, too. He wears a catching glove, much like a baseball player's first baseman's mitt, and a heavily padded glove on his stick hand.

The shin pads are much heavier and wider, as you may have noticed, and a goaltender also wears a protective cup, specially padded pants, chest protector, and a piece of equipment that is a combination shoulder pad and arm pad.

A full mask with a head protector on the back is a must for the goaltender. Great strides have been made in the design of the goaltenders' masks. They have improved 100 percent over the mask that Jacques Plante first wore in the late 1950s, when he shocked professional hockey with his inventiveness. The mask has revolutionized the art of goaltending. The goaltender no longer lives in fear of being hit in the face by a puck or stick. The mask allows the goaltender to change his style and move closer to the ice looking for the puck. The fear of permanent injury is gone.

A hockey player should be certain that he wants to play the goaltending position before he asks his parents to make the heavy financial investment in the specialized goaltending equipment. Most youth programs have equipment that can be borrowed for the boy who desires to play this position, and this seems the best way to start.

The lie of a goaltender's stick is usually more upright, but determining the proper lie also depends on the individual's style. If the goaltender plays from a crouch position, he'll be better off with an 11 or 12 lie. If he's a standup-styled goaltender, he'll be more comfortable with a 13 or 14 lie. If in doubt, start with a lie 12. And again, as mentioned above, check the size of your stick. If the shaft is too long, cut it down or, better still, start with a junior-size stick. You'll find it lighter and much easier to handle.

CONDITIONING

Every athlete, amateur or professional, must take care in the development of his body. Strength and conditioning are vital to the success of a hockey player.

The conditioning of a hockey player is a long-term project. It should start on a serious note at age 10 and be a constant thing from then on. In recent years, the Russian hockey players have shown the world that a superiorly conditioned hockey player is hard to beat.

When the individuals on two teams are well matched in ability, it's the little extras that make the difference in the final outcome of a game. The players' physical condition is one of those important extras.

It is important because hockey is such a fast-moving contact sport that the body has to be ready to stand up to the physical strain.

There is a growing demand for well-planned training programs that use weights and are designed to produce stronger players. Most of the exercises with weights should be geared toward the development of the arms, wrists, trunk, and upper body. However, the best time to work on developing physical strength is during the off- season. The day-to-day skating, practicing, and playing provide enough physical exercise for a young body during the winter months.

Ted Green, a long-time professional, is one who has dedicated himself to body development. Green's return to hockey as an active player after having his skull fractured in a stick-swinging incident that left him paralyzed rates as one of the greatest comeback stories in the history of professional sports. Ted showed determination to regain the use of his arms and legs and went on a daily physical training program that made him one of the most finely conditioned athletes in the world.

A good lesson can be learned from Green's dedication to rebuild his body. When you are young, start doing daily sit-ups, push-ups, and chin-ups. See figures 4, 5, and 6. They are good off-ice activities that will start your muscular development.

FIGURE 4. Sit-ups improve muscle tone. They can be done off the ice also.

FIGURE 5. The push-up helps develop strength in forearms and upper body.

FIGURE 6. Do the exercise properly to reap the proper benefits.

From this stage you can advance to a weight training program, but be sure to work within your limits. It's best to get in a closely supervised program at school. A youngster who overextends himself can be seriously injured.

You can condition yourself at home by taking an 18-inch section of broom handle or broken hockey stick shaft and attaching a weight with a piece of rope on it to the shaft. Then roll the rope around the shaft with your arm extended. This is a great exercise for developing your wrists and forearms, and it can be done easily at home.

A lot of hockey players ask what they can do out of season to keep in good physical shape. Naturally, running is a good conditioner. Although you don't use the same muscles in skating that you use in running, it does strengthen your legs and will help your wind.

Don't show up at a tryout or training camp huffing and puffing and trying to keep up. Do the road work in the summer. Tennis is helpful, and so is bicycling. The Russian hockey players are very big on soccer as a way to keep in shape. There is a great deal of running involved in the game of soccer and it also develops teamwork.

A goaltender should also run to keep his legs in shape and do the regular calisthenics the other players use. But he should limit his weight lifting and concentrate on activities that will improve his reflexes. Ping-Pong is a good game for a goalie. Others recommend handball and squash because in addition to sharpening up the eyes they speed the reflexes and are good for building the legs and stamina.

I am very high on the game of street hockey as an ideal conditioner for the game of ice hockey. I have watched the National Street Hockey championship, played in the Boston area, with teams coming from as far away as Toronto to participate. There aren't many major changes in the rules of the game. The only thing that is different is that you use roller skates on a street or non-ice surface.

Street hockey can be played within the confines of a rink or any enclosed area that is at least 100 feet long and 50 feet wide.

It's a good development tool for the young hockey player for one simple reason. When a player is beginning to learn the game of hockey, he concentrates primarily on his development as a skater so that it's very hard for the other parts of the game to fall into place. Street hockey allows a boy to develop his puck-handling skills, since the game is played with a specially designed ball that doesn't bounce. It also teaches him to look around to see who might be open to take a pass.

Street hockey is a great way for a coach to develop positional play. A coach can put his instructions on a chalk board or spend valuable time on the ice explaining this aspect of the game, but it still takes time for the idea to sink in. In a street hockey situation, the coach can walk through his instructions. When a beginner doesn't have to concentrate hard on his skating, he has time to start thinking about where he should be and how he should work the street hockey puck to an open teammate.

There are great conditioning benefits from the game because the player is always running. A team needs at least a couple of sets of defensemen to keep up the pace.

And the rules of street hockey vary only slightly from those of ice hockey. There is a center line but no blue lines. The center line replaces the blue line so that an attacking player can't precede the puck over the center line. This obviously limits floating and forces an emphasis on team play.

The other difference is in the penalties called by the referee. There are still tripping, elbowing, charging, and so forth, in this game, but instead of sitting the offender in the penalty box for two minutes, a penalty shot is awarded to the offended player.

For this purpose, a penalty shot is placed 25 feet in front of each net. The shooter has the option of firing a shot at the goaltender from that line or walking in to attempt to draw the goaltender out of position.

There are other areas that must be covered with regard to conditioning. Proper diet and rest must be a part of your program.

As you get older, you'll gain weight. Be sure it's good weight and not excess baggage. If you are five pounds over what should be your normal playing weight, you are skating around with a five-pound bag of sugar or flour attached to your back. It slows you down.

Everyone requires a different amount of sleep to be properly rested. When you are tired you don't perform as well as you should. If you feel tired all the time, chances are you aren't getting enough rest.

When training camp or tryouts start, be prepared—but don't overextend yourself the first day. Remember that some of the muscles you are using haven't been used for weeks. Aim to be in the best of condition when the season starts.

If you aren't properly prepared physically for the hitting part of the game of hockey or if you attempt to go too hard in the beginning, you'll be running the risk of injury. An injured player isn't much help to his team.

It's necessary to loosen up at the start of a game or practice. It may be wise to do a few stretching exercises in the dressing room before you get your equipment on, although you could do them when you are dressed and ready to go.

In professional hockey, teams go out on the ice for 15 minutes to loosen up their muscles prior to the start of a game. If your muscles aren't loose you'll develop pulls and tears that will put you out of action.

Youth league hockey players aren't given the 15-minute warm

up, so you have to care for your own needs. If you have started to loosen up in the locker room be sure to follow through with some stretching and bending drills once you get out on the ice. Take it slowly at first until you feel yourself getting warmed up.

For goaltenders, stretching exercises before going on the ice are a must. Once the warm-up period starts, have the shooters warm you up by taking long shots. This will help to develop your reflexes, timing, and confidence. You have to get the feel of the puck.

There is one other note of warning that must be sounded while on the subject of conditioning—that involves smoking, drinking, and involvement with drugs. It has been proven medically that such involvements impair your health, and, therefore, must be avoided.

SKATING

Professional hockey scouts have one basic question when they go out in search of talent—can the boy skate? To use their term, they want to know if the player has the "wheels" to move on his skates.

The name of the game at all levels of hockey is skating. The surest way to attract the attention of a coach is with a smooth striding style that helps you generate great speed.

The quicker you learn how to skate, the faster you can get involved in the actual playing of the game. And I might add that if you are having trouble skating, don't think that you should be a goaltender because at that position you won't have to do much skating. A goaltender has to skate as well as a forward or a defenseman if he is going to excel at his position. Good examples of this are Gerry Cheevers and Tony Esposito. Both are excellent skaters, and this is one of the reasons they rate high as goaltenders.

Once you have been taught the fundamentals of skating, the rest is up to you. It takes a lot of time and effort on your own to develop as a skater. You'll always hear stories about the great stars who skated morning, noon, and night as youngsters. Phil Esposito claims he never bothered to take his skates off for lunch or supper. He had to get back out on the ice. Most of these stories aren't exaggerated. It's this kind of determination and effort that leads to the development of a young hockey player.

You can look at the various professional players and see that they all skate with slightly different styles. Some will be bent over as they glide, while others are straight-up skaters. There are players with short, choppy strides, and classic skaters like the Big M, Frank Mahovlich, who generate great speed with long, smooth strides.

The pros all do the necessary basics of skating the same way. You'll notice that their knees are bent, their weight is slightly forward, and their gliding motion comes from their hips and not their knees. A young hockey player must develop a stride. See figure 7.

From this point the development starts. Don't stand up straight. Keep your knees bent to give you balance, and try to get the feeling that you are pushing off the inside of the blade of your skate. Push off with the right skate and then the left.

I have often noticed teaching beginners to skate at this point in your development you'll have a tendency to start to run on your skates. You may feel that you are in a race to get to the other end of the rink. This is to be avoided. A beginner must develop a stride; speed isn't important.

There are two schools of thought on developing a hockey player. There are some, who I hope are a minority, who claim that you should skate for a year or two before you ever have a hockey stick in your hands. I feel that you will develop quicker and have more balance and self-confidence if you start to learn to skate with a stick in your hands. If you are going to be a hockey player, the stick is one of your tools and it should become an extension of your hands and arms.

As you get into the starting position to skate, your weight is equally distributed on the balls of your feet. Have your toes pointed out slightly. To get started, take three or four quick, choppy steps as if you were running and then start a gliding motion. Push off the inside edge of the blade on your right skate and then the left. Be sure you get the feeling that you are digging into the ice with the inside edge of your blade.

Once you start to get the feeling of striding, a good drill is to skate around the ice without lifting the blades of your skates off the

FIGURE 7. Skating requires you to bend your knees and lean slightly forward.

ice. This will force you to use your hips to develop a skating motion. Power is generated by swinging your hips laterally.

Generally, you will go in a straight line if you have the striding idea down. Remember that you push off your back foot while bringing the other foot forward. And keep pushing off the inside of your blade. The harder you push, the faster you will go. It's not the faster you push that gives you speed, it's the harder you push. As I mentioned before, short, choppy strides should only be used for a quick start.

When you are starting quickly, you must bend a little more from the waist. As the stride lengthens, your body will straighten up a little bit. Think of your start in terms of a sprinter on the track team. He is in a three-point stance starting out, with his body forward. When he breaks from the starting blocks, his upper body is still forward, but once in stride he is more erect and running freely for the wire.

Your skating start is similar in that it takes you a little while to develop your normal gliding motion. A quick start is a must. Many players have been limited in their development by an inability to start quickly. The lack of a quick start has always left them a step or two behind the play.

To get the most out of your stride, the leg you are pushing off of should be extended at the knee with the blade of the skate dug into the ice (figure 8). The good skater is taking his next stride before he gets the full power from the previous stride.

Your right skate blade is almost at a right angle as you push off while you are gliding on your left blade. Your weight is over your bent left knee at this point in your skating stride. Now quickly reverse your position as you move into your next stride. The left blade should be at a right angle and the inside of that blade will be digging into the ice. Your left knee straightens and your weight now shifts to the right skate, which is now the glide skate. Your arms aid in skating by going to the same side as your glide leg and shifting with your body weight from side to side.

Turning or cutting right or left equally well is something that has

FIGURE 8. The push off the right skate provides the power.

to be developed. You may find that most of you can easily cut and turn while skating to the left. It becomes more difficult when you reverse directions and have to go to your right. It's important to be able to turn both ways when playing hockey.

There are two types of turns for a hockey player to learn, the skating turn and the coasting turn.

In both situations there are a couple of basic rules that must be followed. When turning, always place your weight on your inside skate and be sure to lean in the direction you want to go. When I say lean, I mean drop your shoulder in the direction of your turn.

The coasting turn is used to change directions when speed isn't vital. It can be a very sharp turn as you reverse directions. To do this turning right, for example, you lower your right shoulder and lean in that direction. The outside edge of your right blade is digging into the ice as you turn and your right knee is bent, handling most of your weight. The sharper the turn, the more you lean in the direction you want to go.

For a skating turn or cutting turn you have to cross one foot over the other. When crossing over, keep your weight on the inside skate (figure 9), have your knee well bent, and bring your outside leg around and cross it over your inside leg (figure 10). Your body must lean well in the direction of the turn. To develop speed, push off hard with the outside skate, using the inside edge of the blade, and as when striding, dig it into the ice as you push.

When you go skating, be sure to work on developing your stride but don't always skate in the same direction. If you find it harder to cut to your right, spend more time going in that direction until you reach the point where it doesn't matter which way you cut.

Once you are able to move in a straight line and turn corners, you'd better learn how to stop, or you might spend the rest of your life skating around the rink in a big circle.

There is one simple lesson in stopping. You must turn your body at a right angle to the direction in which you are skating (figure 11). As you do this, dig the blades on your skates into the ice to halt your motion, and always lean back slightly (figure 12). You almost feel as if you are going to sit down in a chair quickly and get up right away.

FIGURE 9. In crossing over (cutting) note all the weight is on the left skate.

FIGURE 10. Swing the right skate over in front of the left skate to cut sharply.

FIGURES 11, 12. Notice how the blades of the skate dig into the ice on stopping.

There are two ways to stop. The first, as mentioned above, is with two skates. Remember, for a quick stop, turn your body sideways, dig the blades of your skates into the ice, and lean back slightly.

To change direction more quickly, you will want to learn to stop on one skate. It's similar to stopping with two skates in that the blade must be dug into the ice.

If you want to stop quickly and change directions, something a forward must do almost instinctively, use your front foot. You can also stop on your back foot, which is best for backchecking purposes. Here, all the weight is on your back skate, with your other skate off the ice. The free skate swings around in the other direction and gets you moving quickly. As with learning to cut, be determined to learn to stop in both directions. Work with both feet.

Skating backward is something every player must be able to do, but it has added importance if you plan to be a defenseman. To do this, your knees are slightly bent and a little closer together, and your toes must be pointed in. Your weight should be on the balls of your feet, and you should be bent slightly at the waist so that you are leaning forward. If you are standing in this position you naturally start to go backward.

Skating in this direction is similar to skating forward. You must develop a good gliding motion, pushing off the insides of the blades of your skates. The hips come into the skating motion. If you were to push off from the left side, your hips and weight would naturally shift over to the right side. This is the motion you must develop. Push off one side and let your hips go in the other direction.

When you are skating backward, always skate with your head up and have your stick extended in front of you in one hand. Keep the blade of the stick on the ice, and you will be naturally in the proper position to face an oncoming opponent.

Turning while skating backward must be developed. It's like turning when you are skating forward, because you must lean in the direction you want to go and bring the outside skate over in front of the inside skate. Your weight is on the balls of your feet.

For example, if you are skating backward and you want to turn right, lean your body weight to your right side. Then bring the left

FIGURE 13. It's important to lean in the direction you want to go. Be sure all the weight is on the left skate and bend the knee to maintain balance.

leg over (crossing over in front), and at this point the outer edge of the blade on your right skate is digging into the ice. Don't jump at this point in your turn. Make it a smooth crossover, with your weight eventually coming on to your left skate. To get speed, push off the inside edge of your left skate. Do the reverse to turn left.

To stop while skating backward, point your toes out and dig the inside edges of your blades into the ice. Lean forward to avoid losing your balance.

It's also helpful to be able to stop with one skate while moving backward. Turn in the direction you want to stop and dig the inside edge of the blade into the ice. Your body should lean away from the direction you are moving.

There are a number of good drills that will help you improve your skating. The drills are designed to help you with your balance and to give you flexibility and stamina. If you are working on your own, skate figure eights every chance you get. This simple drill will give you the opportunity to skate in both directions. Don't coast around the turns. Work on crossing over, and remember to lean in the direction you want to go (see figures 10 and 13). Cut down the size of the figure eight to improve your cutting.

A stop-and-start drill is always good. You can skate the length of the rink stopping at the blue line, red line, and far blue line. And be sure that when you participate in such a drill that you stop to the left one time and to the right the next.

A variation could have you starting on the goal line and skating as fast as you can to the red line. Stop, change direction and come back to the blue line. Stop, change direction and skate to the far end of the rink. This is a great conditioning drill, and it gives you special work in the areas of stopping and changing direction.

To develop power, pair off with another skater. One player should push his partner to the other side of the rink. The player being pushed should face his partner with his feet apart. Now dig your blade into the ice and make your partner work hard to move you across the rink. Reverse positions coming back.

To improve turning, skate around the face-off circle five times in one direction and then stop and go five times in the opposite direction. It will help to do this drill skating backward, too.

While skating slowly, pull up one knee and then the other to help improve your balance. Raise one knee and place the stick just over the knee. Then, using your arms and shoulders, pull the knee vigorously toward your chest. Repeat the pull to the chest, then lower the leg and do the same exercise with your other leg. You will be stretching your groin muscles and at the same time giving your arms and shoulders exercise.

Try the leg drag (figure 14). While skating at medium speed, bend one leg at the knee, keeping the other one as straight as possible and trailing behind. Hold the stick at the end in one hand. Lean over, and point the stick straight ahead on the ice. Keep the other hand hanging at your side to simulate catching or blocking a puck. Make sure to keep your head up and look ahead. This, too, will aid your balance, stretch the groin, and help develop flexibility.

Knee bends have always been a favorite drill of mine. This exercise is aimed at strengthening the ligament, tendon and cartilage areas. With your feet fairly close together and coasting slowly, squat down and bounce several times in a deep knee bend.

A leg kick is helpful for stretching and balance (see figure 15). Skate forward slowly. Hold the stick out about arm's length and at

FIGURE 14. Be sure to fully extend the trailing leg and keep your head up when doing the leg drag exercise.

FIGURE 15. Keep the leg straight and kick it up to the level of your stick. Alternate one leg and then the other.

chest level. Kick one leg and then the other to touch the stick. Be sure to keep the kicking leg as straight as possible. A slight variation could have you extend the stick and lift your knees one at a time to touch the stick in front of you. Try to bring your leg up so that your thigh is parallel to the ice and the lower part of your leg is at a right angle to the thigh and upper body.

Running sideways will help you build endurance, power, and maneuverability. You begin this exercise at one end of the ice and run on an angle toward the other end. Keep your skates flat on the ice and your body facing straight ahead. Keep your shoulders parallel with the nearest wall. And don't look in the direction you are moving.

The important thing to remember as you attempt to develop as a skater is to *concentrate* on what you are doing. Don't go through the motions when you are at a practice session. Strive to improve your skating at all times. As I have emphasized before, skating is the most important part of the game.

PASSING AND PUCK HANDLING

There isn't any question in my mind that puck control is the weakest part of a young American hockey player's game. With time and effort, the skating part of his game will shape up. But give the same boy a puck and tell him to skate with it, and you'll quickly discover that he has to learn to skate all over again.

For this reason, I strongly recommend that when you are working on your skating drills, you carry a puck with you at the same time.

The Russians spend hours working with the puck. They handle the puck and pass it better than most professionals. It doesn't happen by accident. It's the result of hard work.

As you develop your puck handling and passing ability, be sure that you have a stick that fits your needs. The hockey stick is an extension on your hands and arms. Always hold the stick firmly with two hands (figure 16). A player who tries to play the game with one hand on the stick soon learns that he is going to be losing control of the puck or giving the puck away on a regular basis.

I once had a coach in high school, John Gallagher, who used to threaten the players on my team. He told us that he was going to tape our lower hand on the shaft of the hockey stick to be sure we used two hands on the stick. He never did, but it emphasized the importance of keeping two hands on the stick. It is just as impor-

FIGURE 16. Hold the stick firmly with both hands.

tant to be sure to keep the blade of the stick on the ice at all times.

The stick should be held in the fingers of your hands. Many young players make the mistake of gripping the stick with the palms of their hands, which limits your ability to control the puck.

Your top hand should grasp the stick firmly just below the nob on the stick, while your lower hand should be between 12 and 18 inches down the shaft. Your hands should be about 12 inches apart when you are carrying the puck or passing it. The bottom hand moves lower down the shaft when you shoot the puck.

The most important thing to remember is to always have the same grip when you are carrying, passing, or shooting the puck. The game moves so fast that you don't have time to change your grip. Keep the stick held firmly in your fingers with your thumbs wrapped around the shaft.

If you are a left-handed shooter, your right hand will be the upper hand. For a right-hander, this is reversed.

Always keep your head up while carrying and passing the puck (figure 17). You have to see where you are going and what you should be doing when you have possession of the puck. Like the other phases of the game, passing and stick handling take particular skills which can be developed through repetition. The ability to pass and receive a puck is a must.

Hold the puck out in front of you while you are getting the feel of it (figure 18). Have your arms extended. Start moving the puck from side to side (this is called dribbling the puck) while standing still. Get the feel of the puck on the end of your stick and try to keep your head up. If you have the puck in front of you, you'll be able to catch a glimpse of it. For better puck control, tilt the blade of your stick toward the puck as you move it from side to side.

Phil Esposito let me in on a secret once when he told me that when it looks as if he is carrying the puck with his head up, he steals a quick little look to be sure the puck is where it should be on his stick. The professionals don't drop their heads to see the puck, they just lower their eyes for a quick glance—and only when they are not quite sure where the puck is.

FIGURE 17. Keep your head up when handling the puck. You have to be able to see what is happening around you.

FIGURE 18. Always keep the puck in front of you when you carry it.

It's important to keep the puck in front of you as you skate with it. Carrying the puck to the side gives an opponent an advantage. He'll know in which direction you plan to skate or to pass the puck. Another drawback is that if you lose possession as you carry the puck it's quickly behind you.

You'll find under similar circumstances that with the puck in front of you, you can regain possession of the puck without breaking stride. If you mis-dribble the puck when it's in front of you, there is an excellent chance that you'll only have to turn your skate blade sideways to kick the puck forward several feet to a point where you can resume carrying the puck with your stick.

Stick handling becomes an important skill as you carry the puck up the ice on attack. See figures 19, 20, and 21. As you stick-handle toward a defender, you are really trying to get him to make the first move. You want him to lean in one direction so that you can go by him on the other side.

As you approach the opponent, fake to one side to get him moving in that direction, and then quickly break in the other direction. To make a fake to the right, move your head in that direction, drop your shoulder, and bring the puck to the right side, too. Your weight at this point will be on your right side, with your knee bent so that it looks as if you are leaning in the direction you want to go.

Quickly reverse directions, when the defender makes a move toward you, by pushing hard off the inside edge of the right skate and quickly moving to the left. Bring the puck with you, being sure to keep your body between the opponent and the puck. You only need a half step to get inside a defender. Don't coast at this point. Take a couple of short, choppy strides to break free.

Don't become a one-way hockey player when you are carrying the puck. In our example above, we have you faking right and going left, but develop your skill to the point where you can fake left and go right with the same ability.

Another way to get around a defender, without faking him, is to slide the puck underneath his stick and between his skates, while quickly moving around him to pick up the loose puck.

If given a choice when making a move to break by a defender, it's to your advantage to fake to your backhand side and then draw

FIGURES 19, 20, 21. Carrying the puck through the cones with your head up is an excellent drill to develop your stick handling.

the puck around on your forehand so that you are in position to get off a shot or make a good pass to a teammate breaking toward the net. However, you'll find as you advance competitively that the defenseman, given the choice, will always try to force you on your backhand. And if you are getting into a one-on-one situation, the good defenseman is going to play your body and check you off the puck. He will play the man and not the puck. For this reason, great time and effort should be spent working on this part of the game.

The best way to practice puck control is by stick handling around the rink, using the side-to-side dribble. At the same time, you can practice head and shoulder fakes in one direction while moving the opposite way. Practice this at medium speed, remembering always to keep your head up.

As you develop this skill, work on a quick wide dribble. Control the puck in front of you and then move it as far as you can to one side. This move is made to the backhand side. Then take the lower hand off your stick and use it to fend off the defender as you move by him into position.

Don't overhandle the puck when you should be passing it to an open teammate who is free and clear to receive a pass.

This brings us to another skill which needs to be developed—passing. Knowing how to give or take a pass is important, but just as important is the ability to know *when* to pass.

One rule that must be emphasized in passing is always lead your man. Pass to the spot where you think your teammate's stick blade *will* be as he breaks up ice at full speed. Don't pass *to* him, because if you do, you'll find the pass in his skates or behind him. Try to lead him so that he skates into the passed puck without breaking stride.

How do you pass the puck in this manner?

Passing the puck requires a long sweeping motion of the stick along the ice, with a follow-through. Look at figures 22 and 23. The blade shouldn't leave the ice. If it does, you'll find that your pass will lift off the ice and be a bouncing puck when your teammate tries to collect it.

It's best to make your passes short and crisp to the open man. Be

FIGURES 22, 23. When passing the puck keep the blade of your stick on the ice.

FIGURE 24.
Be ready for a
pass. Have the
blade of your stick
cupped to catch
the pass.

sure to look before you release the puck. And don't try to make long wing-to-wing passes, which can be easily intercepted.

If you are on the receiving end of a pass, have your stick in the ready position on the ice and have the blade cupped or tilted in the direction from which the pass is coming (figure 24).

You'll have to develop a feel for catching a pass. In addition to cupping your stick, you'll have to be able to release your stick a bit from the impact. Your stick has to give a little bit to allow you to control the puck so relax your lower hand a bit to soften the impact of the puck. It's the same principle as catching a baseball. Your glove always moves away from the ball when the ball hits your glove hand.

If the pass is in your skates or behind you, you'll have to stop and make an effort to control the puck. If the pass is in the air, use your hand to knock it down in front of you as you continue to skate. Don't close your hand on the puck. Just develop the knack of knocking the high pass down.

It's good practice to get yourself a partner and pass the puck back and forth to develop some feel for this art. Eventually you'll be able to skate up and down the ice making short crisp passes to each other.

There are various ways of passing the puck but the one normally used is the forehand pass. It's a lot like shooting a wrist shot although the long sweeping motion is made and always keeps the blade of the stick on the ice. Don't slap at the puck. You'll sacrifice accuracy and your teammate who is the intended receiver will have difficulty handling this type pass.

I must repeat that passes should be made firmly. A soft pass is often intercepted.

The backhand pass (figure 25) is very similar to the forehand pass in that it's a sweeping motion. Be sure to keep the follow-through of your blade along the ice so that your pass won't leave the ice.

The fact that you may be called upon to give off a forehand or backhand pass emphasizes the need to carry the puck in front of you

FIGURE 25.
To make a good backhand pass, sweep your stick along the ice and follow through with the blade low to the ice.

as you skate up the ice. If you have the bad habit of carrying the puck on the side, you'll only be able to pass in that direction; and everyone in the rink will soon learn it is one of your shortcomings.

There are times when you will have to make a flip pass. This is a pass that must be flipped over an opponent's stick in order to reach the intended receiver. The flip pass is accomplished by moving the puck out onto the end of your blade (figure 26), called the toe of the blade. With a slight rotating motion of your wrist, you'll be able to lift the pass over any obstacle which may be between you and an open teammate (figure 27).

The drop pass has two variations and it is the type of pass that should be used chiefly in the attacking zone. One drop pass requires that you leave the puck sitting motionless for a trailing teammate. The other is a drop pass with a tail that allows you to slide the puck back as you skate toward the net.

The drop pass is a dangerous pass. You must be sure that you are

FIGURES 26, 27. The flip pass is made by placing the puck on the end of your stick blade and rotate your wrist up as you shoot.

FIGURES 28, 29, 30. The boards become a teammate when properly used. Notice how the attacker played around the defender by using the boards.

leaving the puck for a trailing teammate. And when you leave the puck for him, be sure that you continue to skate at the defender, screening him off the puck and setting up your teammate for a shot. At the same time, you'll be screening out the opposing goaltender and should be preparing yourself to move in on a rebound if it develops.

Another consideration in puck handling and passing is the proper use of the side boards. See figures 28, 29, and 30. There are many times during the course of a game when you'll be able to deflect a pass off the boards even though there is a defender between you and your teammate. If you can't make a direct pass, feel free to use the boards. It will help you move the puck to the open man.

You'll have to develop a knowledge of the boards of the rink you are playing in. Are they alive or dead when the puck hits them? That is, how well do the boards deflect a pass? And at what angle should you pass the puck to get it to your teammate? In most cases, try to keep the passes low when you are banking a pass off the boards.

There are a few rules you should remember when thinking about passing as part of the game of ice hockey.

1. Never pass the puck without looking to see where you are sending it.

2. Avoid making passes around your net. Work the puck to the corner or to an area of limited pressure before releasing the puck.

3. Avoid passing the puck from wing to wing in your defensive end. And you have to be careful when making a lateral pass close to the blue line in the attacking zone because an alert defender will pick off the pass and have a good break up ice.

4. Don't pass the puck to a teammate who isn't open. The puck carrier who head-mans or advances the puck up ice to an open winger who is skating alone ahead of him is a true team player. He isn't trying to do it all himself. He's working with his teammate and there isn't a better way to move the puck than to head-man.

5. Don't be content to merely pass the puck. Put the pass on your teammate's stick.

SHOOTING

The object of the game of hockey is to score goals, and if you don't shoot the puck on net, you can't score a goal.

There are some who will neglect this phase of the game and claim that goal scorers are born, not made. I can't agree with this kind of thinking. Developing your shot will make you a better goal scorer, and any player who can consistently put the puck in the net is an asset to his team.

The basic attributes of shooting and scoring have always been accuracy and power. But another important aspect is quickness. There are many players who shoot the puck harder than hockey superstar Phil Esposito. Bobby Hull is a perfect example, and so is Bobby Orr. But even with their great shots, they have never developed the quickness that has made Esposito one of the greatest scorers in the history of the game.

There are many different kinds of shots. Some players rely on the slap shot, while others go with the wrist shot. There are snap shots, forehand and backhand, plus flip shots to consider, too.

The different shots are used for different situations. They must be quick and, most importantly, on the net.

How do you shoot the puck?

You can start by gripping the stick firmly and sliding your lower hand down the shaft of the stick. See figure 31.

The blade of your stick should be tilted slightly toward the puck, and, depending on the type of shot you are trying to make, the puck should rest on a definite part of the stick blade. A wrist shot will require that the puck be somewhere between the shaft end of the stick and the middle of the blade. The flip shot requires that the puck be on the tip or toe of the stick blade.

A young hockey player should work to develop a wrist shot. It is most important because it offers accuracy. The better one develops his wrist shot, the more goals he'll score.

The *wrist shot*, sometimes called a forehand shot, begins with a sweeping motion that starts behind your body (figure 32). Slide the puck back along the ice 15 to 18 inches, and then, with the blade of your stick cupped over the puck, you are ready to fire your shot on net (figure 33).

FIGURE 31. Slide your hand down the shaft of the stick to shoot the puck.

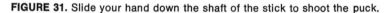

FIGURES 32, 33.
The wrist shot starts
with a sweeping motion
toward the target.

FIGURE 34. Notice the shift of weight from the back skate to the front skate while shooting.

FIGURE 35. Look up when shooting on net.

Taking this shot is a bit like hitting in baseball. If you are a right-handed shooter, your left shoulder will be facing the target. A hitter does the same thing. The right-handed batter will have his left shoulder aimed right at the pitcher. Having your shoulders aligned properly will help you to always have your stick blade following through on target.

You'll develop power in your shot by learning to shift your weight properly from the back skate to the front skate (figure 34). It's something that has to be worked on in practice, although a good player is capable of shooting off of both feet.

For our example, a right-handed shooter would be pushing off his right foot and transferring all his weight to his left (front) foot.

Get the rhythm down for pushing off the back foot and shifting the weight to the front foot. At the same time, you will be sliding the puck toward the target. And as the weight shift develops, snap your wrists, putting some power in the shot.

The fact that all your weight is on the front foot is an asset in that you will be better prepared to take a body check—being hit by an opponent while in the process of getting your shot off.

You control the height of the shot with your follow-through. If you want to keep the shot low or along the ice, keep the blade of the stick right on the ice as you complete your shot. To lift the puck, open the blade of the stick and turn your wrist up as you follow through.

You must learn to shoot with your head up (figure 35). The shooter has to know where the goaltender is and pick a spot. Later in this chapter we'll discuss where the best spots to shoot for are.

Don't keep your eyes glued to the puck. Just take a quick peek at the puck before you shoot to be sure that it's where you want it on the blade of your stick. As soon as you drop your head to look at the puck, you are giving the goaltender the signal that you are planning to shoot. That is why it's necessary to develop the ability to shoot with your head up. When you practice shooting, glue your eye on the spot where you want to place your shot, and you'll be amazed at the accuracy you'll develop.

The *slap shot* is the most overrated shot in the game. Too many young players waste time and effort developing a hard slap shot

FIGURES 36, 37, 38. The timing of the weight shift from the back skate to the front helps put muscle in the slap shot. The blade of the stick hits the ice a few inches behind the puck.

that usually makes a loud booming sound as it goes wide of the net and hits the boards or glass.

Certainly there is a time and place for the slap shot in a game. But it's the last thing you should be working on when you are trying to improve your shooting. The slap shot reduces two important aspects of shooting the puck—accuracy and quickness.

How do you slap the puck?

The principle is similar to the wrist shot. You shoot the puck from the forehand side. You slide your bottom hand down the stick shaft a little lower, and you wind up a bit, bringing the stick back and up about waist high (figure 36). From this point, you release your muscle into the shot (figure 37). The weight shift is the same as for the wrist shot, with the weight being shifted from the back foot to the front foot at the time your arms and shoulders are about to make contact with the puck (figure 38). The blade of the stick hits the ice about two inches behind the puck and just continues to drive right through the puck in a slapping motion. You control the height of the shot with your follow-through. If you want to keep the shot low, keep the blade of the stick along the ice as it heads in the direction of the target.

The one major difference in making the slap shot is that you have your head down when you take the shot, just like the golfer keeps his head down when he's trying to hit that little white golf ball.

You can take a slap shot when you are skating, too. In order to do this, push the puck a few feet in front of you and move into the shot. Be sure your body resembles the baseball batter as you get ready to hit the shot. It takes a little more timing to get this shot down, but it's the most powerful shot you can make.

Bobby Hull just blasts away at the puck when he winds up his slap shot, and there isn't much a goaltender can do if the shot is on net. It will be traveling well over 100 miles per hour from the 30- to the 50-foot range.

The shot I'd recommend is a *snap shot* that has been made popular by Phil Esposito. It's somewhere between the wrist shot and a slap shot. The snap shot is more powerful than a wrist shot and quicker and more accurate than a slap shot.

So if you combine its added power with quickness and accuracy, you can see that it's something you should work on.

Quickness is the key to this shot. Esposito tries to have his shot on net before the goaltender knows he has the puck.

The puck is shot from the middle of the blade, and as with the other forehand shots, the weight shift is important.

The major difference is when you start the shot. The wrist shot requires that you slide the stick back along the ice. The slap shot has you bring the stick back off the ice about waist high; any higher is too high and takes too long to get the shot off. In the snap shot, you bring the stick back off the ice as in the slap shot, but instead of bringing it back waist high, pull the stick off the ice only six to eight inches (see figure 37). Now snap the shot off quickly and follow through.

The *flip shot* is used in special situations. The puck is placed out on the toe of the stick blade. The lower hand slides down the stick shaft a little lower than normal. And to flip the puck up into the air, you just rotate your wrists in an upward motion and follow through high.

It takes a little time to master the flip shot, but it is very useful around the net when the goaltender is down across the goal line. You want to be able to flip the puck up over him to score a goal.

There are defensemen, such as Jim Dorey, whose teammates call him "Flipper," who will carry the puck to center ice and loft a flip shot several feet in the air in the direction of the opposing goaltender. The puck will take some crazy bounces when it lands; and therefore, it's a useful means of putting the puck in the other team's end if you don't have an open wing to receive a pass. I'm sure you have seen goals scored this way.

The same kind of shot can be used by a defenseman in his own end to relieve pressure. If you don't want to ice the puck—shooting it the length of the ice—forcing a face-off in your own end, by flipping the puck out of trouble, you can relieve the pressure and allow your teammates time to regroup.

The *backhand shot* is getting to be a lost art. When professional players started putting curves in the blades of their sticks, the use of the backhand was restricted.

If you have a straight blade on your stick, you should work on a backhand shot. It will be useful around the net. But if you have a big banana hook in your blade, forget it. There is no way you'll be able to control the puck and get the backhand shot off properly.

You use more of a sweeping motion with the stick when taking this shot (figure 39). You start with the puck well behind your body and then move a little lower to get your body into the shot. Slide the puck along the ice in the direction of the target, with your weight shifting from the back foot to the front, and get a little snapping motion into your shot with your wrists.

There is an element of surprise for the goaltender when a player takes a backhand shot. It's usually hard for the goaltender to figure out where the shot is going to go.

Another plus in being able to make a backhand shot is time. If the puck comes to you on your backhand side and you can release a fast shot, you have added quickness. If you get the puck in the same spot and have to shift the puck over to your forehand, it might be that split second or two that will allow a defender to make a move with his stick or body on you and cause you to miss a chance to put the puck in the net.

Forwards have to develop the knack of deflecting shots in front of the rival goaltender. To deflect a shot, you have your back to the

FIGURE 39.
Be ready to slide your hand down the shaft of the stick and use a sweeping motion to make a backhand shot.

49

FIGURE 40. Keep your stick on the ice in front of the net and try to stay clear on the defense to be in position to deflect a shot on net.

net and face the shooter. Be strong on your feet as you gain good position in front of the net and be sure to keep your stick free and clear. Now you are in position to change the direction of the puck with the blade of your stick as the puck is shot at the net. See figure 40.

The deflection is usually impossible for the goaltender to stop. He probably will have already committed himself to the original shot when you tip it and send it in the opposite direction.

Another important item in the shooting game is picking the best spot to place your shot as you fire at the net.

Know where the goaltender is before you fire the puck. Don't make him look good by firing the puck into his pads.

There are four open corners of the net when the goaltender is standing in the middle of the four-feet high by six-feet wide cage.

The toughest shot for the goaltender to stop is one that is low to his stick-hand side. The next most difficult shot to save is fired low to the glove-hand side.

In fact, low shots are the hardest for the goaltender to stop, so be sure when putting a shot on net that you follow through with your stick blade low to the ice to keep your shot down.

If the low shot isn't available to you as you move in on goal, then shoot high to the stick-hand side. Your fourth and final choice should be a shot high to the glove-hand side. It's reasonable to assume that most goaltenders are going to have good hands and will be able to pick off most shots to the catching glove side.

Tony Esposito is a flopping goaltender who is never afraid to go down when a shot is directed at him. For this reason, some people in professional hockey claim that Tony is weak on high spots. "They may be right," said Tony one day when talking about goaltending, "but you can't prove it by me. I keep a record at home of the types of goals I give up over the course of the season. And in the end, I always give up more shots that were low on net than were high shots."

You should know if you are facing a right-handed or left-handed goaltender before the game starts. Know which is his stick side, so that if you get a good scoring chance, you will know right away where his low stick side is. Scoring chances develop and die so quickly that you won't have a lot of time to think about these things. Know beforehand where you are going to shoot the puck if the opportunity arises.

One other bit of advice about shooting. In basketball, coaches always tell a player to follow his shot to the basket in case the shot is missed. This puts him in position to collect a rebound. The same principle is true for a hockey player. Follow your shot to the net. Don't take a shot and then turn away from the net. Get the rebound if the goaltender gives the puck back to you.

You'll find that the great goal scorers have more than a little knack with the puck around the net. They all have great determination to score.

Quickness, accuracy, power, and determination will help you become a great scorer.

KNOWING YOUR JOB

What is the right position for you? Should you be a center, wing, defenseman, or goaltender?

Only time will tell which position you are best suited for, because there are special skills involved in playing every position.

A big, strong player who doesn't have quickness should probably think about being a defenseman, while a fast skater will be of more use up front as a center or wing. In hockey, the center and wings are often called forwards.

It's helpful to develop as a complete player. You can accomplish this by becoming a student of the game and learning everyone's job. In this way, you'll be able to step into any situation that might develop.

CENTER

I have always felt that the best hockey player on the team should be the center. He must be a strong skater who is a good stick handler, passer, and puck carrier. In addition, the center must have an added sense—the ability to anticipate what is going to happen next on the ice.

To a degree, the center is like the football quarterback who must read the defense as he comes up to the line of scrimmage.

The center in most offenses is the primary forechecker. He is quick to move at a defender with the puck in the attacking zone. This is called forechecking and it's a move designed to force a defensive mistake to create a scoring chance. He has to be on the puck all the time and anticipate where the play is going next.

If some other player jumps ahead of the center into the attacking zone, the center must be quick to realize what is happening and cover his teammate's position in the attacking zone. If the first man on the puck is the right wing the center should take over that position in the zone. If it's a defenseman he should drop back to defense. This is the primary reason a center must be thinking all the time. He must be aware of everything that is going on around him.

The center, in most cases, will be the individual around whom the offense revolves. He'll be the man the puck goes to in the middle as the offense moves up ice, and he'll control the play as the puck moves into the attacking zone. He must know where his wingers are and be aware of when they are open or free. It is his job to develop a play to get the puck to them.

The center, or any other player carrying the puck up ice, should quickly size up the situation. Are you breaking up the ice alone? Do you have a three-on-two jump?

It's at this point that you as center must develop the attack. You might work on one defenseman and try to spring a wing free. If the wing is trailing a bit, cut when you get inside the blue line. The wing should know what to do by what the center does. If you cut toward the wing, you usually drop him a pass and continue skating toward the defenseman, whom you can then block out of the play.

If the center breaks away from a fast-closing wing, he'll take the defenseman with him. This tells the wing to go straight for the net, because that's where the center is going to put the puck for him.

Face-offs are almost exclusively handled by the center. A consistently good face-off man can be the difference between a winning or losing team.

Quickness on the face-off is a must. It also helps to have strong wrists and forearms to get control of the puck.

FIGURE 41. Always be ready in the face-off circle. Watch the official's hand for the drop of the puck.

You'll be called upon to take face-offs in the neutral zone, attacking zone, and defensive zone (figure 41). You'll have different ideas on which direction you are trying to draw the puck depending on where the face-off is called.

The most important face-off is the one that comes in your defensive zone. You *must* stop your opponent from winning the face-off here. If you don't, you are allowing the other team a good scoring chance.

Most centers will try to draw the puck against the center they are facing. A good center will even draw the puck toward his own net, if he feels the opponent is going to draw the puck toward the boards. If you have this tendency, you should talk it over with your goaltenders so that they'll know what you are going to do when you line up to take a face-off.

If the face-off is on the left side, and if the opposing center is a left-handed shooter, it's natural for him to draw the puck toward the boards.

The center always controls the play as he is moving into the face-off circle. You should look first to be sure that your teammates have lined up properly. The center should spread his feet apart a little wider than shoulder width. You must have a firm grip on your stick and lean forward a bit, keeping your eyes glued on the referee's or linesman's hand to watch for the dropping motion as he releases the puck. But as the center you are the one who determines go. The puck won't be dropped until your stick is in place at the face-off circle. So get comfortable and in a ready position before you put your stick down.

Some centers will try to out-guess their opponent. Watch your opponent's feet to get an idea of which way he's going to try to go with the draw.

If the shooter is left-handed and his right skate is closer to the face-off line, he'll probably be trying to draw the puck back toward the boards. If he has his left foot near the line, he'll probably be trying to make a shot off the drop of the puck.

There are times when you may feel quicker and more comfortable taking a face-off if you slide your hands down the shaft of your stick a couple of inches—the way a hitter chokes up on his bat in baseball.

Getting back to a defensive face-off, try to get the puck back to a defenseman, who can take it behind the net and watch the forwards set up for a break-out play.

Late in the game when you are protecting a one-goal lead, the center's job isn't merely to win the face-off, but to be sure not to lose the draw.

That may sound like a contradiction, but it's part of knowing your job as a face-off man. In this situation in your own end, you want to be sure that your opponent doesn't get the puck back cleanly to a shooter who is ready to unload a shot on your net. In this face-off situation, you want to play for a tie.

Use your strength to tie up the opposing center and the puck. You do this by moving into the opposing center with your stick and body as the puck is dropped. Try to tie him up. Don't let him get his stick on the puck. Move your stick underneath his so he can't get to the puck.

Of course, in the attacking zone it's a different situation. A good center will work to get the puck back to a defenseman at the blue line (point) or to a wing standing behind him on the face-off circle near the slot.

The center has the option of drawing the puck in the direction of either of his wings, or trying to take a shot.

Phil Esposito has a great move he makes using his size and strength for face-off situations in the other team's end. Once or twice during a game, you'll see him forget the puck at the drop and concentrate on lifting the opponent's stick off the ice and away from the puck with his own stick. At the same time, Esposito will start to skate in the direction of the net, collecting the puck with his skate blade and kicking it in the direction of the net so that he's able to make a shot on the rival goaltender.

It's obviously helpful for a center to develop a quick and accurate shot around the net. A good center uses his body to get clear position in front of the net and pounces on rebounds.

WING

The wing's job varies from that of the center, because he is more restricted in where he should go on the ice. We have already divided the ice surface lengthwise from end to end into three equal parts.

The middle section is the center's lane, while, obviously, the right wing patrols the right lane, and the left wing on the left side.

The wing basically goes up and down his lane or "street." He can move into the center lane, too, but should rarely be found roaming on the far side of the ice in the left wing's street.

If the puck is in the right corner and the right wing is on the puck in the attacking zone, the center should back him up along the boards while the left wing moves in front of the net.

The forwards form an "L" in this situation. The left wing, or the man in front of the net, should not park in front of the net. He should move around a little bit to make it harder for the defenseman to cover him. He must be sure to keep his stick on the ice and try to get body position so that he can collect a pass from the corner and get off a quick shot.

Having the self-discipline to stay in his own lane is a must for a wing. When he starts roaming all over the ice, both the offense and the defense break down. Positional play is an important part of the wing's job. It also helps for a wing to have good speed, a hard shot that can be taken while skating at full speed, and the size and muscle to work hard battling for the puck along the boards and in the corners.

Normally, a right-handed shooter will play right wing and a left-handed shooter will play left wing. It's easier to catch a pass and give a pass on your forehand, and it's also helpful to be on your forehand as you break for the net to take a shot because you have more power with a forehand shot.

There are exceptions to every rule. The legendary Maurice "Rocket" Richard of the Montreal Canadiens was a left-handed shooter who played right wing. The one advantage for Richard and others playing the off-wing is that they have a better angle to shoot at as they move toward the net from off the wing, because the puck is on the inside of the body.

The Russians have strong feelings about having their players skate the off-wing. They feel that the percentage for shooting on net is definitely better. But they are more skillful and handle the puck better than most players from other countries, and, usually with a straight blade at the end of their sticks. For this reason they have little trouble controlling a pass on their backhand side.

Probably the most important duty of the wing is to learn how to break in properly from the blue line to the opponent's net. The first few strides from the blue line are the most important. If you receive a pass while cutting toward the net, you must be aware that it's the defenseman's job to skate you off the shooting angle.

Therefore, break directly for the net when you get the puck and take your shot while you have a good shooting angle.

If the defender gets position on you, he'll drive you right out of the play.

You only need a half step to have position on an opponent as you skate toward the net. Once you have your hip inside the defender (figure 42), get strong on your skates by widening your stance, and move at the net with the puck. Because you have a defender on

57

you, there probably won't be an opportunity to unload your best shot at the goaltender, but you should be able to put the puck on net. It has a chance to go in if the shot is on net. A by-product of your ability to get position on your opponent is the pressure it puts on him to attempt to stop you. In many instances he'll draw a penalty and your team will be on the power play.

Like the center, the wing must be aware of everyone else's job during the course of play. If the center is out of position forechecking, the nearest wing must jump right at the puck carrier and try to force him to make a mistake in his own end.

If a defenseman on a wing's side of the ice rushes the puck, he must check to be sure that either the center drops back to cover the defenseman's chores or do it himself.

Naturally, backchecking is an important part of the wing's job.

FIGURE 42.
Once you get the half step on a defender you are in control and should move right for the net. He'll have to hook, hold or trip you to prevent a good scoring chance.

The center and wings must be able to adjust quickly to offensive situations that develop as they break up ice into the attacking zone. Is the puck carrier one-on-one, two-on-one, two-on-two, three-on-two going against the opponents' goal? What do you do under the developing circumstances?

One-on-one pits the puck carrier against the defender, who is usually a defenseman. The defenseman has one basic rule to follow in a situation such as this. He should forget the puck and play the man. If you are the attacking player, it's your job to force him to make a mistake. Try to make him commit the first move with a head and shoulder fake or a quick, wide draw.

Don't skate directly at the defenseman. Move at him just outside his body so that he's forced to move toward you, rather than you going directly at him.

Perhaps the best move is to tease him with the puck as you dribble it. Show him the puck and try to get him to lunge at it. When he commits himself, pull the puck back and cut in the opposite direction of his lunge.

If you are unable to force a mistake, you have a couple of other options. You can try to take a shot, or you can take a quick look back to see if one of your teammates is breaking up ice alone.

If you have a trailing wing, slow down a bit as you go over the blue line and move directly at the defenseman, while at the same time dropping the puck for the trailer. It's then your job to block the defenseman off the play.

The next situation is the two-on-one break. In this situation, work hard to develop one good scoring chance. Don't overhandle the puck, as you skate into the attacking end. Every time you make an extra pass, you are increasing your chances of making a mistake—because for a pass to be completed, it takes somebody to pass the puck properly and a teammate on the wing to catch the pass correctly. If either fails in his responsibility, the play will be broken.

In the two-on-one break, the puck carrier brings the puck wide of the defender, trying to open up a lane that will allow him to skate right in on goal to take a shot. The other option is for the puck carrier to draw the defenseman toward him. Once the puck carrier has the defender committed, he can make a quick pass to a teammate who should be alone some place in front of the goal.

Remember, don't over pass the puck. Look for that one good shot.

The two-on-two break is similar to the one-on-one in that it's a limited opportunity to score. It takes teamwork between forwards who know each other's moves to develop a good scoring break, unless the defenseman makes a mistake.

It's best to try to confuse the defenders by having the puck carrier cut in front of the defense. With luck, his checker will come with him as he crosses in the other direction. This will force the second defender he is skating toward to make a move in his direction, too. At this point, the puck carrier drops a pass for his trailing teammate.

The only other variation, other than a drop pass and some sort of a screening effort by the original puck carrier, is for the puck carrier and wing to try to work on one defenseman.

Here the puck carrier moves toward the defender on the same side as his breaking wing. He's trying to force the defenseman toward him, while attempting to pass off to a wing breaking behind the defense.

When the three-on-two situation develops, coming out of your own end, it is best to work the puck to the middle, where the center should be skating his lane. The wings must discipline themselves to stay wide on their respective sides. If the left or right wing drifts toward the middle, the defenseman has a chance to play both the center and the wing at the same time, because they will be too close together.

The puck carrier now moves toward one defenseman and tries to get him to commit to the puck. He then slides a pass to his wing breaking behind the defenseman, who has been drawn toward the puck carrier.

If the puck carrier can't force a mistake on the part of a defenseman as he skates toward the net, he must take a shot. At the same time, both wings should break for the net, looking for a rebound.

Another option suitable for this type of break up ice is for the center to pass the puck at the blue line to his right wing. The right wing stays wide, trying to draw the defenseman toward him as he skates into the corner.

The center slows down and moves into a position 25 feet in front of the net, in the slot, while the wide left wing breaks directly for the net. The second defenseman will usually go for the left wing who is heading for the net, thus setting up the center alone in the slot for a return pass. The situation can be reversed, with the center skating right at the net to draw the defensive coverage, and the wide left wing moving into that slot area 25 feet out, looking for the centering pass. The key is for the wing who becomes the puck carrier to stay wide and draw the defenseman toward him. Obviously the situation reverses when the center passes the puck to the left wing and the right wing becomes the wide wing.

The duties of the defensemen and goalies will be discussed in the sections on checking and goaltending.

CHECKING

Hockey is a physical game, and strength is an important asset for a hockey player.

You want to be able to use your body, not only to check and be checked but to get good position on your opponent.

Russian hockey players have great physical strength. They play a well-disciplined checking game that takes advantage of this strength.

But the word "checking" has a dual meaning in the game of hockey. Certainly, to use your body to hit an opponent is checking, but there are times when you check an opponent and there is nothing physical about your assignment.

I'm talking about the important skills of forechecking and backchecking. It takes a two-way effort on the part of an individual to forecheck in the attacking zone and then recover when the opposition gains control of the puck to start backchecking.

I have spent a great deal of time describing the offensive part of the game, with instructions on skating, puck handling, passing, and shooting. At this point, I want you to become a complete player and think of your defensive assignments as well as your offensive thrust when you are on the ice.

Forechecking is more often than not the responsibility of the center. But there are times when this duty can fall to the wings or even to a defenseman in the rare case when he is the first man into the attacking zone or the nearest man to the new puck carrier when the opposition gains control of the puck in its own end.

Most teams have their assignments in the attacking zone set up for the center to do most of the forechecking. But there are exceptions to the rule. The Boston Bruins had a great scoring line of Phil Esposito at center with Ken Hodge at right wing and Wayne Cashman at left wing and this line always let the wings forecheck in the corner.

Hodge and Cashman were so big and strong that they could gain control of the puck in the corners and pass it back to Esposito standing in the slot 15 or 20 feet in front of the net. This is one of the reasons Phil was able to have a 76-goal season one year. His wings owned the corners.

If you are the center and it's your assignment to forecheck but somebody else is in there first and doing the job, you must back up your teammate and play the position he would normally play.

A good forechecker reacts quickly to the situation. He wants to try to force a mistake in the opponents' end of the ice. The center or any other player who assumes the responsibility of forechecking should not skate directly at the puck carrier. Approach him from an angle.

If you skate directly at the puck carrier you are actually giving him an advantage. He'll fake one way and go the other way on you. Take advantage of the boards and limit the ways he can move. Give him the boards and then use your body to take him off the puck. Just step into him and separate him from the puck.

A skilled pro will at times play the puck while forechecking, knowing that if he misses the puck he'll take the man out of the play.

The surest way for a beginner to handle such a forechecking situation is to play the man. Don't let him advance with the puck on the play. Go at the man with your stick extended in front of you (figure 43). Look at the man, not directly at the puck. You will still be able to see the puck.

If the puck carrier is behind the net, you have to be ready for two possibilities. If he swings wide and attempts to take the puck up

FIGURE 43. When forechecking go right at the man with your stick fully extended.

the boards, you must move with him and use your body to skate him into the boards. If the puck carrier decides to fake to the outside and come up the middle of the ice, you, as the forechecker, must stop on your outside skate and step into the puck carrier with your body (figure 44).

Another situation in the attacking zone that calls for you to use your body is when you are going after a loose puck in the corner or along the boards. Don't let an opponent get to the puck first. Go right after the puck with him and use your body to get between him and the puck (figure 45). You will then be in position to set up a scoring play for one of your teammates. Your team will have control of the puck.

There is one very important message to be conveyed as we discuss backchecking: Always skate faster coming back into your own defense end of the ice than you do when you are on offense.

Backchecking is basically the job of the wings. But if a wing is caught deep in the attacking zone, the center has to move over to the unprotected side of the ice and help out by covering an open man.

FIGURE 44.
Be sure to get your body between the puck carrier and the puck to separate him from the puck as a forechecker.

FIGURE 45.
Along the boards get your body between the opponent and the puck to gain control.

65

A good backchecker helps to make a defenseman's job easy. Backchecking also helps to limit the number of scoring chances on your goaltender. And the fewer the chances on your net, the better your chances of playing for a winning team.

How does a backchecking wing help the defense?

A wing who comes back and picks up the open attacker on his side of the ice allows his defenseman to stand at the blue line and concentrate on making a play on the puck carrier. He doesn't have to worry about a pass being made to an open wing.

You should start thinking about backchecking when your team loses possession of the puck in the attacking zone. It will only take a little bit of actual playing in the game for you to realize at which point you shift gears from being an offensive-minded player to a defender.

Once a player on the other team has possession of the puck and starts to look around to make a move out of his defensive end, you had better look for the man you are supposed to check and start skating back up ice to pick him up as quickly as possible. Don't let him break up ice alone.

When backchecking, always match skating stride for skating stride with your check, keeping a stride ahead of him, and keeping yourself between your opponent and the puck. This will have him skating into your end of the ice along the boards. Follow him all the way to your net if that's the direction he is headed. Don't give him an opening so that he'll be free to get the puck.

You'll have to glance over your shoulder occasionally to see where the puck is, but it's important for you to stay with your check until your team has possession of the puck and is ready to break up ice on the attack.

A word of caution: Don't be a halfway backchecker. I have watched many lazy hockey players, even at the professional level, who will pick up their man and follow him back to the blue line. At this point they fall asleep, forget they are playing defense, and make a quick loop toward the boards, looking for somebody to give them a pass so they can go on offense again. Meanwhile, their check comes up with a solid scoring opportunity.

The hitting part of the defenseman's game is almost a lost art in today's open game. The last of the good bodycheckers in the National Hockey League was probably ex-Bruin Leo Boivin. He had that knack of moving into the puck carrier and knocking him off the puck with a solid hit, using his shoulder or his hip.

Bobby Orr, Brad Park, and Pat Stapleton came along and changed all that. They are offensive-minded defensemen, who are more adept at controlling the play and moving the puck out of their own end than they are at checking an opponent out of the rink. Orr revolutionized defensive play with his great ability, but there is still a place in hockey for the solid bodychecker.

The shoulder check and the hip check are two means of hitting an opponent. But don't get into a habit of going out on the ice and hitting every player in sight. There is a proper time to use the body. A defenseman has to be in a man-on-man situation to step into an opponent.

To shoulder check your man, crouch a little bit and come up at his chest with your shoulder. You straighten both legs as the hit is made and try to take a step through him to knock him off balance. The power comes from your legs as you make the hit. The shoulder check (figure 46) is most commonly used on a player who has his head down.

Timing is the key to hip checking. You'll be trying to hit the puck carrier as you skate backward. You have to get down low, and as he attempts to skate around you, you slide into him with your hip (figure 47). It's best to use this check on a player who is trying to get by you on the way down the boards. He won't be able to get away from your check.

It's best not to try a hip check on a player in the middle of the ice. If you miss, you'll allow him to skate in alone on your net.

In a one-on-one situation in the center-ice area, you should always try to skate the puck carrier off the angle. Once you have done this, be sure to stick to him to make sure he isn't free to make a pass and set up a scoring play. To do this, press him against the boards using your hip and arm to tie him up.

The stick is also used to check an attacking player. The poke check and the sweep check are necessary skills. The stick is merely an extension of your arm. When poke checking, hold the stick in

67

FIGURE 46. If the puck carrier has his head down shoulder check him by putting your shoulder right into his chest.

FIGURE 47. To hip check, get down low and step into an opponent.

FIGURE 48. The poke check is a sudden thrust forward with the blade of your stick to knock the puck off the opponent's stick.

FIGURE 49. Hook the puck from the opponent with a sweeping motion to sweep check.

FIGURE 50. Lift the opponent's stick off the ice to prevent him from controlling the puck. This is most important in front of your own net.

front of you as the opposing player skates down on you (figure 48). When he comes close enough, give a firm jab with the stick at the puck on the blade of his stick and knock it free. You step at the player while making the move with your stick. Let the man come to you, don't commit yourself too soon or he'll give you a fake and go right by you. Perhaps the best poke checker in the game at this time is J. C. Tremblay who played with Montreal and later with the Quebec Nordiques.

J.C. was a perennial all-star who never ran an opponent off the ice with his body checking. He used his stick effectively, and let the puck carrier get to the perfect spot where he could make that one step and poke the puck clear.

The sweep check is a dangerous maneuver that should be used very sparingly by young players. It's a judgment move, and if it fails it will pull you out of position and allow the attacking player clear sailing.

To sweep check, you hold your stick in one hand. Most of the best sweep checkers in the game will switch hands to get the best swipe at the puck with the hand nearest the puck carrier. Let the man come to you with the puck, just as in poke checking, but try to approach him from an angle instead of head on. When he gets near enough, bend the knee nearest the puck so that your stick is extended flat on the ice and hook the puck away from the puck carrier (figure 49).

The stick can be used to lift an opponent's stick off the ice (figure 50). Just move in close and place your stick under his stick and lift it quickly. Then bring your stick back to the puck, and you have gained possession.

Don't forget that defensive hockey is played by everyone, not just the defensemen.

GOALTENDING

The goaltender is the most important individual on a hockey team. He has to be capable of carrying the load when the rest of the team hits a flat spot. As somebody once said, goaltenders don't win games, they only lose them.

That is the kind of pressure a goaltender must live with when he's on the ice. A forward or a defenseman can make a mistake and nobody will know the difference. If a goaltender makes a mistake, the other team is on the scoreboard, and everybody in the rink knows why.

It takes a particular type of athlete to be a goaltender. The first rule is that he must be an excellent skater. Other requirements for the position are: self-confidence, perfect eyesight, good reflexes, coordination, the desire needed to be a good competitor, and size.

Some people argue that goaltenders come in all shapes and sizes. But from my experience the perfect goaltender is the good rangy player who doesn't have a tendency to be heavy. A lean goaltender has more quickness.

The game of hockey has changed a great deal over the past decade. The ability to cover a greater area of the net, which I think is greater in a large player, is more important now than the quickness that a smaller goaltender usually has. Hockey, with its curved sticks and booming slap shots, is a shooters' game. There aren't too many players who show finesse as puck handlers and goal scorers.

There are two styles of goaltending. The classic stand-up goaltender was Jacques Plante. He rarely left his feet, and he concentrated on cutting down the shooter's angle.

In recent years, younger players such as Tony Esposito who go down on the ice to block shots have increased.

What is the best style for you? That's something you'll have to decide as you work at the position.

I have a preference for the stand-up goaltender. Once a goaltender is down, he doesn't have complete control of the situation in front of the net and seems to be always scrambling to recover.

All goaltenders, whether stand-up or up-and-downers, spend many hours developing an ability to play the angles.

A shooter can come in three directions toward the goaltender standing in front of the net. He can skate straight on, break in off the wing, or move out front from the corner or behind the net. A goaltender must be ready to react under all circumstances.

The goaltender must start by standing in the crease area in front of the net. Develop a comfortable stance as you stand in the middle of the net.

The stand-up goaltender is more erect. He has his weight on the balls of his feet, his knees bent slightly, his back arched forward from the waist, his stick on the ice, and his glove hand in a catching position at his side.

The up-and-down goaltender follows the same basic rules, except that he crouches more, and this naturally causes him to lean forward just a bit more.

If you get in your ready position standing on the goal line (figure 51), you give the shooter the maximum amount of net to shoot at. He has equal room to your left and right.

You can cut down the angle by moving out a few feet toward the shooter (figure 52). You cut down the angle because the shooter who is skating directly up the middle toward you can see less net to shoot at than he could with you back on the goal line. The more you move out of the net toward the shooter, the less he has to shoot at. You

FIGURES 51, 52. Look before shooting at the goaltender. Pick a corner for your shot. Notice the difference when you play the angle. The goaltender in figure 51 is back in the crease giving the attacker plenty to shoot at. In figure 52, he has moved out to cut down the angle and reduce the scoring chance.

FIGURE 53. Learn to move in an arc from post to post to cut down the angle without losing your position in front of the net.

are really playing the percentages cutting down the angle and using your body to block the shot.

The up-and-down goaltender tends to do just the opposite. He doesn't move at the shooter in the same manner. He gets way out on the angle and starts to back in as the shooter approaches the net. It's a matter of preference.

As you make your move to stop the shot, you should always have your eye on the puck and be in the ready position to make a save. A shooter can fire on net at the most unexpected times.

Don't worry about the puck carrier's body as you get ready to make a save. Play the puck. Line yourself up with the puck.

It takes a little learning to get the feel of how to work the angles on a puck carrier coming in off the wing. See figure 53. Visualize an arc from post to post and stay on the arc. A good rule to remember in this situation is to never give the shooter the short side. The short side is the side nearest the post. If you obey this rule, you give a puck carrier breaking off the wing only one area to shoot at, and you know where he has to put his shot—to the far post.

Your stick is an important tool, and the blade of the stick should be on the ice at all times. If you relax when the puck is in the other end of the rink, keep your stick blade on the ice. If you want to straighten up, just slide your hand up the shaft of the stick a bit.

Many goaltenders overlook the value of using the stick effectively. You can use the stick to poke check the puck from an opponent. This becomes necessary when you have a puck carrier walking out from behind your net or from the corner.

Another must in this situation is the necessity of keeping your body firmly against the near post (figure 54). Make sure there isn't an opening for the puck to slip between your body and the post.

The stick is necessary to clear the puck. You'll have to learn to shoot the puck like a forward. It takes practice.

The goaltender must have good movement in his crease area.

FIGURE 54. When the puck is in the corner be sure you are firmly against the post.

FIGURES 55, 56. To go from post to post turn your lead skate in the direction you want to go and then quickly bring your pads together ready to make the save.

When the puck goes from one side of the net to the other, he must have quickness coming across the mouth of the goal.

To come across the mouth of the goal, turn one skate in the direction of the play and push off hard from the inside edge of the blade of the other skate (figure 55). You'll have to dig that blade edge into the ice to get the push it will take you to get to the other side (figure 56).

There are times when you are out on the angle as a puck carrier moves across the front of the net. If he is moving slowly or is 30 or 40 feet away, you don't want to rush to the other side of the net. In this situation, move slowly with him, keeping your eye on the puck. As you side-step, always be sure to bring your pads back together. For example, if you want to move to the left, take a short side step with your left skate and then bring your right pad together with your left.

How far apart should your legs be? It's best to have your feet about shoulder-width apart. This leaves a slight opening between your pads. But they are close enough together for you to close them quickly if the puck is fired directly at them.

There are times when you don't have a lot of time to move from one post to the other in order to make a save. When a situation requires that you get to the other side of the net as quickly as you can, you are going to have to make a two-leg slide. See figures 57 and 58. The puck carrier is in close to the net in this instance, and you have to move with both pads together as quickly as possible in the direction of the puck. It's a lot like a slide in baseball, only you must have one pad above the other to prevent the puck carrier from shooting the puck over into the net. And be sure to keep the lower pad flat on the ice so the shooter can't slide the puck under you (figure 59).

Keep your top hand above your body as you slide toward the puck. You never know when the puck is going to hit you, and as a goaltender you have to be willing to stop the puck any way you can.

You'll find that your glove is your best friend. But don't get in the habit of trying to catch every shot that comes in your direction. If a shot is low to the glove side, use your pad or stick to make the save. Don't get caught reaching while the puck goes in the net because you have relied too much on your glove hand.

FIGURES 57, 58. There are times when you must throw your body across the mouth of the goal to make a save. React as quickly as possible and keep the bottom pad along the ice.

FIGURE 59. The shooting area is reduced when the top pad comes into place to form a higher barrier.

If a shot is lifted on the net and you are planning to catch it, be sure to back yourself up when time permits by moving your body behind your catching hand. In this way you'll have a little insurance against the puck dipping the last minute and breaking off your glove hand. By backing up, you will force the puck to hit your body.

There are times when you will only have time to use your body to block a shot. Avoid giving off a rebound by using your glove hand to gain control of the puck.

If a shot is fired up at your stick-hand glove, use it to make the save and be careful what you do with the rebound. Angle your stick-hand glove so that the puck goes in the direction of the boards and not back to the shooter.

The same rule applies to using your stick. Angle the blade of the stick as you make a save, and send the puck toward the corner. Be sure to keep your stick blade square to the ice when stopping the puck. If you hold the blade at an angle, the puck will skip up over it and probably go into the net.

A goaltender who controls his rebounds can help his defensemen in his own end. If time permits you to stop the puck without giving off a rebound, look for a defenseman and give him the puck. You may have just enough time to deflect the puck in his direction. Or you may have time to put the puck at the side of the net for him to pick up and start a break-out play.

You have to learn to play the puck even when it's off the angle, that is when there is no possible way for the shooter to put the puck in the net from where he's standing unless he fires the puck off you and it gets behind you. This is called "giving up a cheap goal" and it certainly is something you'll want to avoid.

Remember that we said when the puck is in the corner or behind the net you must have your body jammed against the near post with no opening for the puck to slip through. Think about how your stick can help you in this situation.

Use your stick to block a pass-out (see glossary) headed in front of the net by an opponent. Keep it extended in front of you with the blade on the ice. Try to control the pass-out and move the puck behind the net. But if this is impossible, at least deflect the pass-out to change the direction of the puck. Don't let it go directly to an opponent in the slot area.

A skillful goaltender will be able to play the pass-out using the full length of his stick. You still must have your body protecting the near post, but you can crouch down and reach as far as possible to change the direction of the pass-out.

The stick can be used to poke check the puck away from a player who is moving in off the angle. It's too dangerous to try a poke check against a shooter who is coming directly at you. To poke the puck away, the shooter must be coming at you from the same side on which you are holding your stick. Be sure that he commits himself to coming from the same side on which you are holding your stick. Be sure that he commits himself to coming from that angle, and then when he gets close enough, dive at the puck, leading with your stick, and knock it off his stick. Use your body as a backup to your poke-checking effort.

Be ready to handle the rebound off the boards when the puck is shot wide. Use your stick to control the bouncing puck.

As has been mentioned, you have to adjust to particular situations as they arise. The screen shot is the most difficult to stop because it may be difficult to see the shot. In this situation, crouch down lower than normal and try to spot the puck through the bodies and skates in front of the net. It's best to keep your balance by having your weight equally distributed on both legs. Move out to the top of the crease to cut down the angle. And remember the fundamentals—keep your stick on the ice and your glove hand in a catching position to the side of your body.

There are many times when a screened shot will hit your body without you ever having seen the puck. Be quick to cover the rebound in this case. It may be good to get a stoppage of play so that your coach can change his lines, but generally the stoppage will permit your teammates to get reorganized.

I must bring up the point of the catching glove again because there are many young goaltenders who keep the glove hand in front of their body where it does little good. A puck shot at that spot would hit the stomach area. Keep the hand at your side, ready to grab the puck, with the glove in the open position. One day a player will unload a blazing shot you don't see and it will head right into your glove. Your teammates and fans will cheer wildly after this spectacular save, when in truth you will have made the save because the glove was in the right place at the right time.

A goaltender has to be able to handle the high flip shot coming in his direction from center ice. Play the puck, don't let the puck play you. By this I mean that you should move out of the net and catch the puck before it bounces in front and takes a crazy hop behind you. If you can't get your glove on the flip shot, move out of the net and let it hit your body. Get as close to it as you can.

It's not a good idea for a goaltender to roam over the defensive end of the ice. There is a proper time to come out of the net. You'll have to develop judgment as to when you should go after a loose puck that is sliding in your direction. Usually there is an opponent chasing after that loose puck with hopes of skating in alone on you.

You must have much better than a 50-50 chance to get to the puck first. And you won't have much time to make up your mind. If you think you can beat the man to the puck, DON'T HESITATE. Move right at the puck and clear it to a teammate.

If you are a good skater you'll be able to move out of the crease area quickly and stop a puck that has been fired around the net. This helps your defensemen. In this situation, it's best to leave the net and return in the same direction when you move after a puck. It will eliminate confusion between you and your defensemen and avoid a collision.

The penalty shot is a particular challenge to a goaltender. It's helpful if you know the opponent you face. Is he more inclined to shoot the puck than to move in close and try to fake you out of position?

Don't guess. Just be ready as he moves toward the net. Once he touches the puck you are allowed to move out of the crease. Skate out a few extra feet to cut down the angle. If he decides to shoot he really won't have much of the net to shoot at. If the puck carrier decides to move in toward the net, slide back toward the net and be sure to play the puck. Ignore his body fakes.

Remember, your job as a goaltender is to stop the puck. Stay up on your skates as much as possible, and wait for the shooter to make the first move. Learn to control your rebounds and work on your angle play.

A goaltender should function as the catcher for his team. If there is a face-off in your end, be sure your teammates are lined up properly and that they know who they will be covering when the puck is dropped.

It's helpful if you talk to your teammates. Let them know where an opponent is and how much time they have to make their play with the puck. If an opponent is left uncovered in front of the net, give a yell to let a teammate know that he should cover in front of the net.

While you are playing, do not talk unless it's necessary. And most importantly, never criticize a teammate when he makes a mistake that results in a goal.

It's your job to stop every shot fired in your direction. Learn to play the shots one at a time. If you get beat, tell yourself it's the last goal you plan to give up in the game. A goaltender who gets down on himself when he gives up a goal isn't going to be ready mentally to make the next save. And in hockey every save prevents a goal.

BASIC OFFENSE

Hockey is a team game. Individual skill certainly plays a vital part in the success of a team, but in the end it is the ability to play together (the Russian style) that brings the desired result.

There are many theories about how a hockey team's offense should be developed. And there are many factors that must be considered by a coach before he finally decides what will best suit his players' talents. If a team lacks great overall speed and is only average in puck-handling, it would be wrong for that team to develop an attack that emphasized wing-to-wing passing.

When thinking about offense, there is one point to remember at all times: Head-man the puck if you want to make your attack go. Move the puck forward at all times. Move the puck to the open man. You can pass the puck up ice quicker than you can carry it.

The Russian style of play best emphasizes this point. Their great coaching authority Anatoli Tarasov insists that when getting the puck back from the opposition, a player does not start ragging or handling the puck. Instead, he demands that his players quickly pass the puck to a teammate. His point is that the puck moves much faster than a hockey player can skate. Thus the principle of leaving the defensive zone with a pass to a teammate breaking up ice is the main weapon in the Russian arsenal. And it should be incorporated in any team's basic offensive plans.

The by-product of moving the puck up ice with crisp passing is that if everyone on the team tries to move the puck to an open man while on offense, they develop an unselfishness that every coach tries to achieve.

Another part of the Russian thinking on offense that must be viewed favorably is their style of give-and-go. When a player makes a pass, he quickly skates himself into position to take a return pass.

Another important consideration is that you must know what the situation is when your line or defensive pairing is designated to go on the ice. What is the score? How much time is left in the period? Does the opponents' style of play force you to do things differently?

To begin a discussion of offense, let's start with face-offs. All play starts from a face-off, whether you are in the neutral zone, attacking zone, or defensive zone.

The game starts from center ice, and figure 60 shows you where you should be when it's time to drop the puck.

Face-offs in the defensive zone are the most important, so be sure you know how the attacking team is lining up for a face-off before you get yourself in place. Do you have the player you must cover when the puck is dropped in sight?

In figure 61, the puck is to be dropped to the right of the goal-

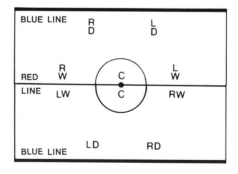

FIGURE 60
FACE-OFFS

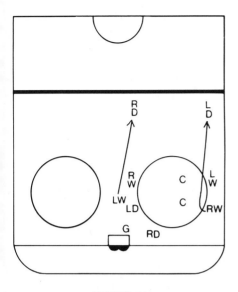

FIGURE 61
DEFENSIVE ZONE RIGHT

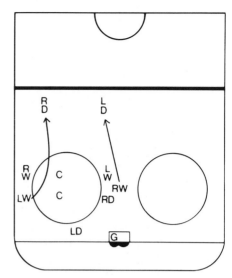

FIGURE 62
DEFENSIVE ZONE LEFT

tender. The left wing must protect against the right defenseman on the point. The left wing must stay clear of traffic so that he won't be bumped by an attacker as he moves out to cover. Always work on the theory that the quickest way from one spot on the ice to another is a straight line. As you look at the diagram, notice that the right wing has a dual job. He must check the left wing. But if the puck goes directly back to the left point, he must adjust his thinking and move quickly in that direction.

The same principle applies to face-offs to the left of the goaltender (figure 62) except that the role of the wings changes slightly. In this situation, the right wing goes directly to the point while the left wing assumes the double responsibility of the opponents' right wing and right defenseman.

There are variations of the basic face-off situation in the defensive zone. Some teams will pull the wing off the boards and put him in a slot behind the center on the face-off circle. In this case (figure 63), when the attacking left wing moves into the slot, the right wing must know where his check has lined up and change his positioning for the face-off, too. The defensive-minded wing moves off the boards, too, and tries to place himself on the face-off circle so that he can move quickly at the left wing. When the attacking team makes this type of an adjustment, it is obvious that they are attempting to draw the puck back to that left wing in the slot. Be aware that the right wing on the attacking team will attempt to screen off the defenders as they move through that slot area. Please note that the defensive right wing in this situation has double responsibility: in addition to moving at his check, the left wing, he must also protect against a face-off that goes back to the left point.

Obviously, the roles of the left wing and the right wing change if the face-off moves to the left of the goaltender (figure 64). Defensemen must also line up differently depending on where the official drops the puck.

During a face-off situation in the neutral zone, most centers will attempt to draw the puck back to their defense to get the attack organized (figure 65). The attacking wing's job is to shield off the opposing wings, so that the defensemen have a chance to look up and make the pass that will put the offense in motion.

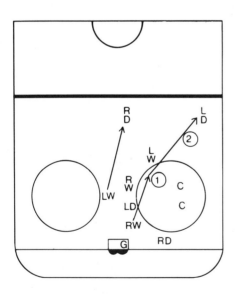

FIGURE 63
DEFENSIVE ZONE RIGHT (SLOT)

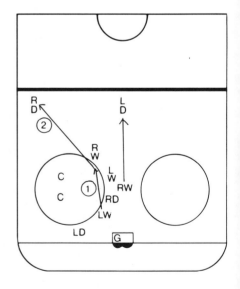

FIGURE 64
DEFENSIVE ZONE LEFT (SLOT)

Normally, if the center gets the puck back to a defenseman (figure 66), he can expect a quick return pass if he can skate himself into the clear. You'll notice in this diagram that the principle of give-and-go is apparent. As soon as the defenseman draws the forechecker, he passes to the open man, who in this case is the center.

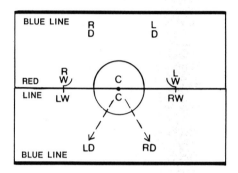

FIGURE 65
CENTER ICE (OFFENSIVE)

Wingers shield off wingers.
Defensemen always over blue line.

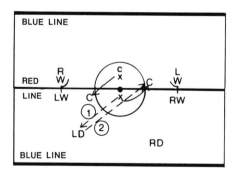

FIGURE 66
OFFENSIVE FROM CENTER ICE FACE-OFF

The basic face-off in the attacking zone (figure 67) calls for the center to draw the puck back to the defenseman on the point. In this instance, with the face-off in the left face-off circle, the tendency of a right-handed shooter taking the face-off would be to draw the puck on his backhand in the direction of the right point. The left-handed center has two options. He can try to work the puck back to the left defenseman, while the center and two wings screen out possible defenders, or he can make a shot off the drop of the puck because he is on his forehand. The center must let the right wing know his intention for two reasons: so that the wing will go right for the net on the drop and try to distract the goaltender by screening him, and so that he will be looking for a rebound.

Variations in the attacking zone will develop. In figure 68 the right wing moves off the boards and the center tries to draw the puck to him in the slot. This is a right-side face-off. The procedure

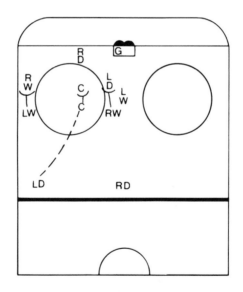

FIGURE 67
FACE-OFF OFFENSIVE ZONE

Center draws to defense—all forwards screen.
Note that center with left shot can shoot—must tell RW to go to net.

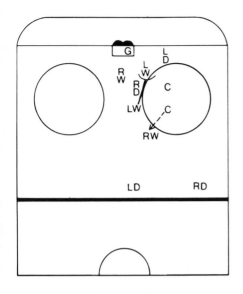

FIGURE 68
FACE-OFF OFFENSIVE ZONE (SLOT)

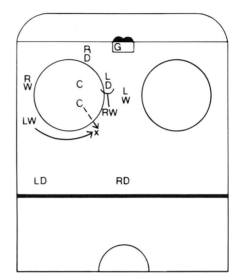

FIGURE 69
OFFENSIVE ZONE (MOVING WING)

is reversed if the face-off is on the left side of the ice. Some teams attempt to confuse the defensive team. In the situation shown in figure 69, the left wing breaks for the slot and the center tries to bring the puck back to that spot. If the right wing shields off the defenseman lined up next to him, the left wing should be able to take a direct shot.

Lining up properly and carrying out defensive assignments becomes even more important when your team is shorthanded. The defensemen must be flexible. For example, in figure 70, the right defenseman is the key man. He must assume the role of a wing if the center wins the face-off back to the left wing on the face-off circle. If the opposition lines up straight across, the defense (figure 71), depending on which side of the ice the puck will be dropped, must also line up straight across. In this situation on the left side of the ice, the left defenseman must be the most alert man on the ice. He has to move quickly in the direction of the puck. If the face-off goes to the opposing right wing whom he is covering, the left defenseman must take him out of the play. On the other hand, if his own center

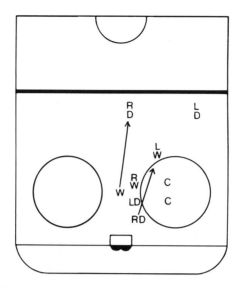

FIGURE 70
SHORTHANDED FACE-OFFS (SLOT)

RD must check slot wing if face-off goes directly to $\frac{L}{W}$ in the slot.

wins the draw back, the defenseman must be quick to jump on the puck and move it out of the defensive end.

Don't forget that when your team is shorthanded you are allowed to shoot the puck the length of the ice. There is no icing when your side is shorthanded.

Another special face-off you'll encounter will come late in a game when your team is trailing by a goal, or in some cases two goals, and your coach decides to pull his goaltender off the ice in favor of an added attacker.

There are two keys to a face-off in this situation. The attacking wings (figure 72) must be sure to screen out the defenders much like a basketball player sets up a pick. Secondly, the center must win the face-off back to the man in the slot. In this particular diagram, with the face-off on the left side, it would be best to have a right-handed center drawing the puck back to the wing on the face-off circle. The man who is being set up for the shot should be a left-handed shooter. The left-handed shooter can handle this type of pass more easily.

Also note how the wide wing on the face-off slips behind the defense, looking to screen the goaltender or pick up a rebound.

Positional play is important as a team develops its offensive patterns. Everyone has to be in his designated area for the attack to work. There are many ways of coming out of your own end. We'll keep to the basic break-out patterns, so that fundamentally you will know what any coach is talking about when he is instructing his team. Some coaches will use different words to get their point across, but they will all be operating from the same basic patterns. Obviously, the more skilled you become as a player, and as the team develops through hard work, the more variations can be added.

Breaking out of your own end is one of the game's hardest jobs. Basically all attacks start with a defenseman standing behind his net with the puck (figure 73). In our diagram, the right defenseman takes a look around to see where everyone is and then starts the play in motion. His job is to draw the opposing center, who in this case is the chief forechecker, toward him and then release a pass to his own center, who will then move toward the middle. Notice how

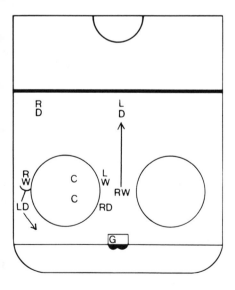

FIGURE 71
SHORTHANDED FACE-OFF

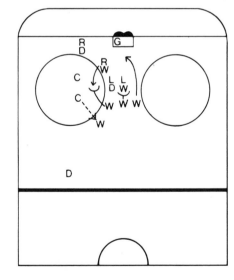

FIGURE 72
SIX ATTACKERS FACE-OFF

the right wing clears the traffic in the area around the face-off circle by releasing from his station on the boards as the play develops. This gives the right defenseman and the center a little room to work.

A variation is the quick-out. In this situation (figure 74), the defenseman catches the other team out of position and quickly hits the open man. This is something a young defenseman must learn to do. Don't take too much time and thereby let the opposition set up their forechecking system. Hit that open man with a quick pass and you are out of trouble. In this instance, notice how the defensive right wing has forgotten his check and allowed the defenseman to move the puck to his left wing.

There are some teams that put a major emphasis on forechecking. They try to force mistakes in the attacking end and will send two forecheckers in deep. When this happens, as in figure 75, the defenseman with the puck must make a quick pass to the open man. Perhaps one of the advantages to the basic system we are using—a system that should be used at the developing levels of hockey—is

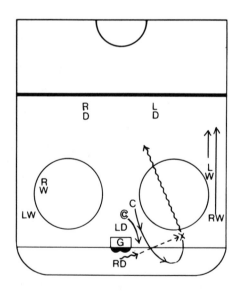

FIGURE 73
OUT OF OWN END (ONE FORECHECKER)

Defenseman draws forechecker toward him.

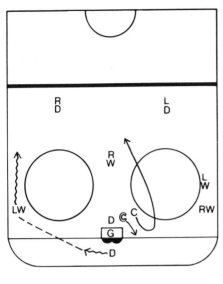

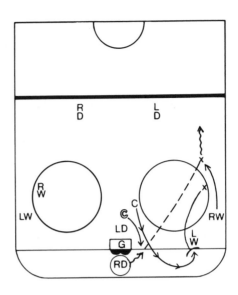

FIGURE 74
QUICK OUT

FIGURE 75
OUT OF OWN END (TWO FORECHECKERS)

Open wing.

that it always calls for a defenseman to be protecting in front of his own net.

Young hockey players make mistakes, but under this system even if a mistake is made there is a safety valve. This is true when two forecheckers are putting pressure on the developing attack. In our example, notice the center moving at the defenseman starting the play, while the left wing moves into position to prevent the center from receiving the pass.

When the left wing moved into the forechecking assignment, this automatically freed the right wing, who should come off the boards into an open area to take a pass from his defenseman. The right wing can't be floating out of the zone. He must move off the boards and position himself near the top of the face-off circle. If he moves too far up the boards, he'll shut off the opening, because the opponents' defenseman will be able to make a play on him.

In this situation, the young defenseman has one safety valve. If the pressure is coming from the opposing center, and your own center is covered, and there doesn't seem to be much of an opening to make the break-out pass, slide the puck around the boards so that your right wing can pick up the play from there.

The professionals are more sophisticated in the many ways that they come out of their own end, but it took them years of hard work to develop their skills and know-how.

If there is a solid forechecking effort underway, often the two defensemen will have to work together to start the break-out. In this case (figure 76), the right defenseman has the puck behind his net, and, from what he sees, everyone seems to be pretty well covered. On a given signal, he'll call the left defenseman into the play. The left defenseman then moves into position in the corner of the rink. He'll usually be unguarded. The right defenseman must move the puck to draw the forechecker toward him. Once that move is made, he slides a pass to the left defenseman, who should have the center open to start the break-out play. You'll notice in this diagram that the attackers aren't bunched together. Everyone is in his own lane ready for a pass.

The variation to this break-out (figure 77) would call for the de-

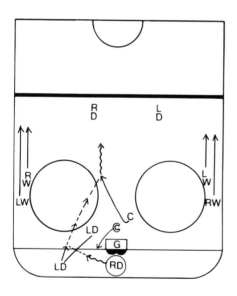

FIGURE 76
DEFENSEMEN START BREAK-OUT

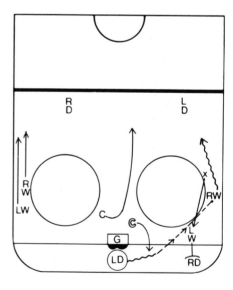

FIGURE 77
OFFENSIVE PLAY

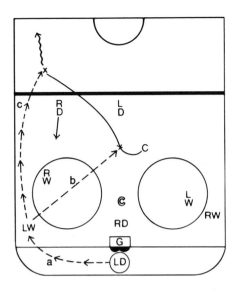

FIGURE 78
LATE WING COVER

a—around boards
b—pass into middle
c—backup option to center

fenseman in possession of the puck to take advantage of the left wing who's jumping in to forecheck against the other defenseman and pass to the right wing. Notice again how the defenseman with the puck has to move from behind the net to draw the center toward him. When he does this, he knows where the opposing center and left wing are, and if his own right wing is playing his position he must be open.

In a situation such as this, a Russian right wing would give a quick pass to his center and then break up ice quickly for a return pass on the give-and-go.

There will be times when the opposing defenseman out on the point will make a move to prevent a break-out play. The team on the attack must take advantage of such a move. In our example (figure 78), which shows some options for the left defenseman as he starts the break-out you'll notice the right defenseman on the opposing team moving in to try to stop the break-out pattern.

What has happened in this diagram is that the left wing is free to take the clearing pass because his check is late getting into the play. The defenseman has quickly moved the puck over to him along the boards. Now the left wing has two options. His check is moving at him. He can hit the center who is starting to swing up the middle or he can delay just a second, drawing that right defenseman deeper into the zone, and then bank the puck off the boards to the center, who is behind the defenseman and on his way to a good jump up ice.

The boards should become part of your individual style of play. There are times when the boards can serve you almost as well as another teammate. Learn to bank the puck off the boards to make a pass to a teammate. Use them to your advantage in a one-on-one situation by flipping the puck off the boards and skating behind the defender to pick the puck up. Always remember that it's very hard to shoot the puck through an opponent and very easy to use the boards to get the puck to the same final destination.

When a young team has the services of a talented player at center, the plan of attack can be developed around this individual. In figure 79 you'll notice that the center swings behind his own net to start the break-out play. He has several options as he starts to move up ice:

(A) He can carry the puck by the forechecker, using his ability to beat the man—although he must be careful not to lose possession of the puck at such a critical point on the ice. (B) He can carry the puck and draw the forechecker toward him and then drop a pass for the trailing defenseman. In this instance, the center must form a screen or pick to take the forechecker out of the play. (C) He could signal for the left defenseman to move over into the left corner as he starts to move behind the net. If he does this and is under heavy forechecking pressure, he can slide a pass over to the left defenseman, who can carry the puck up the left boards. The left wing must be alert to the fact that the play is moving out his side of the ice and move toward the neutral zone. This will bring the defending right wing with him and give the left defenseman clear sailing and time to work the give-and-go back to his center.

Now that you are able to move the puck out of your end, we should consider some of the other situations you will encounter while on offense. Certainly the most basic form of attack is for the team to clear their defensive zone and dump the puck into the attacking zone. Under NCAA rules you only clear your own defensive zone before firing the puck into the far end. In professional hockey, in order to avoid icing the puck, you must clear the red line before dumping the puck into the attacking zone.

In figure 80 the center clears the red line, sees that his right wing is flying, and shoots the puck into the right corner. When the center does dump the puck into the attacking zone, he should be sure to keep the puck wide of the goaltender. In our diagram, the center fires the puck from the left side and uses the boards effectively because the rebound is coming right out to the fast-breaking right wing.

The *two-on-one break* should result in one good shot on net. We have cautioned already against overhandling the puck in this situa-

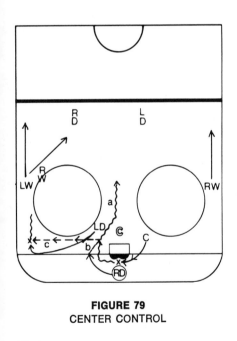

FIGURE 79
CENTER CONTROL

Center
a —carries by forecheck
b —drops for trailing RD who carries
c —waits for LW to clear zone and uses LD to carry

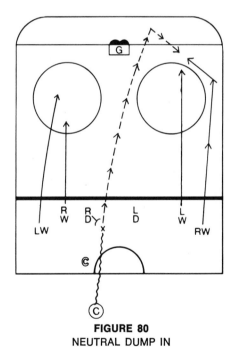

FIGURE 80
NEUTRAL DUMP IN

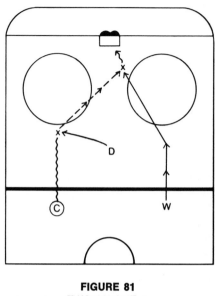

FIGURE 81
TWO-ON-ONE A

tion. In figure 81 the center carries the puck down the left side, trying to lure the defenseman to him, while hitting the wing with a pass as he breaks for the net. If the defenseman doesn't make a move at the puck carrier he must move right at the net and take the shot (figure 82).

The *two-on-two* requires the attacking team to force a defensive breakdown. In figure 83 you'll notice that the center carries the puck over the blue line, cuts right and tries to bring the defender to this side of the ice. At this point, he'll drop a pass for a trailing wing and screen the other defenseman out of the play. In the second instance (figure 84), the center has skated directly at the right defenseman and screened him out of the play, while leaving the puck for the right wing to fire a shot.

The man carrying the puck controls the situation on a *three-on-two*, and it's good for line-mates to remember what a teammate likes to do in a particular situation and be ready to act accordingly.

The center in figure 85 carries the puck over the blue line and moves at the left defenseman, trying to make him commit himself.

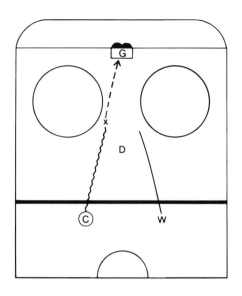

FIGURE 82
TWO-ON-ONE B

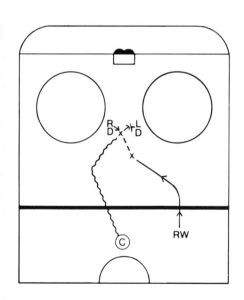

FIGURE 83
TWO-ON-TWO A

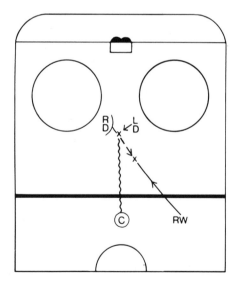

FIGURE 84
TWO-ON-TWO B

If the defenseman does make a move at the puck, the center slides a pass over to the right wing and the right wing moves right at the net. Notice that the left wing skated deep into the face-off circle. He brought the right defenseman with him, and by doing so prevented the defenseman from making a play in front of the goaltender.

In figure 86 the right wing has carried the puck into the attacking zone. He carries the puck into the face-off circle area, drawing the left defenseman into the play with him. The center moves right to the net, followed by the right defenseman, who covers in front of the goaltender. Thus the trailing left wing can move toward the middle of the ice to take a centering pass from the right wing.

The three-on-two can go down the wing wide to set up the center (figure 87) although this depends on how the defensemen react. It's pretty certain that if the right wing carries the puck to the face-off circle, he'll draw the left defenseman with him. If the left wing stays in his lane and skates deep into the face-off circle, he could bring the right defenseman with him. In this case, the right wing needs only to slide the puck over to the center, who should be unguarded in the slot.

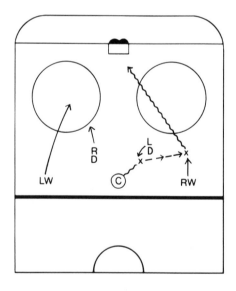

FIGURE 85
THREE-ON-TWO CENTER CARRY

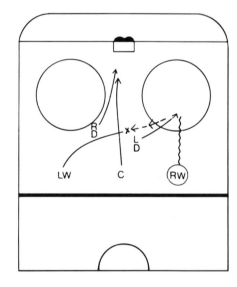

FIGURE 86
THREE-ON-TWO WING CARRY A

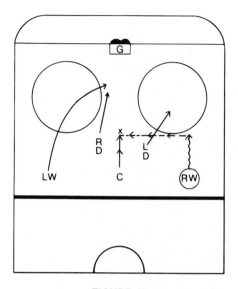

FIGURE 87
THREE-ON-TWO WING CARRY B

As stated earlier, it is the opinion of many hockey experts that the goaltender is the most important member of a hockey team. If that is the case and the object of the game is to score goals, then the most important offensive weapon a team possesses is its *power play*. We'll spend a great deal of time developing the basic idea and duties of the man-advantage situation.

In figure 88 the defenseman waits for the center to skate around the net and then takes the puck and starts the attack in motion. The center must then swing wide and be ready to take a pass. The defenseman's job is to draw the forechecker toward him before he releases his pass to the center.

To reverse the situation (figure 89), instead of leaving the puck for the defenseman, the center circles his net and takes the puck. He must draw the forechecker toward him and then give the puck back to his defenseman, who carries the puck straight up the ice.

The power play really begins to develop in the neutral zone.

You may recall that, in figure 88 the center left the puck for the defenseman and then skated into position to take a pass. In figure 90

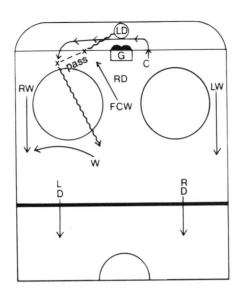

FIGURE 88
POWER PLAY A
BREAK-OUT DEFENSE TO CENTER

Defenseman draws forechecker and passes to breaking center.

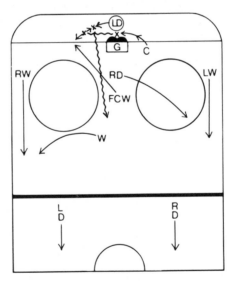

FIGURE 89
POWER PLAY B
BREAK-OUT CENTER TO DEFENSE

Center takes puck, draws forechecker deep and leaves
puck for his defenseman to carry straight up the ice.

the center now carries the puck to center ice at a controlled speed, making sure that his teammates are breaking up ice together. The last man out of the defensive zone is the left defenseman, who started the play. He swings down the left boards, and when he hits the neutral zone he accelerates and breaks for the attacking zone, looking for a clear pass. If you follow the path of the other players you'll notice that the left wing has opened up the lane down the boards for his left defenseman by drifting toward the center of the ice.

The same situation can develop when the center leaves the puck for the defenseman, who then automatically carries the puck up the middle of the ice (figure 91). Again, a set play is in motion, with the right defenseman swinging wide and the left wing bringing any potential defensive wing toward the middle, so that the entire left

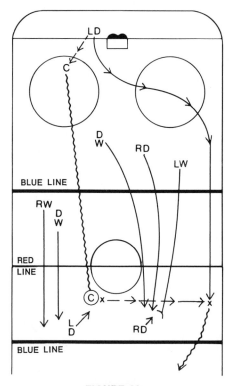

FIGURE 90
POWER PLAY A
NEUTRAL ZONE CENTER BREAK-OUT

side of the ice opens for the breaking right defenseman. There can be adjustments to set up whichever player the coach wants to be the breaking attacker coming down the boards.

Once the puck moves into the attacking zone, the players must have the discipline to play their positions. The key to the success of the play then becomes the ability to move the puck quickly and to try to force an opening in the defending team's armor.

The basic goal of the power play is to set up for a good scoring chance. The defenseman, as shown in figure 92, would like to be able to get the puck into his center in the slot. Notice how the right wing stays wide when the puck is on his side of the ice, while the left wing moves toward the mouth of the goal. The opposite would occur if the left defenseman had the puck. It would then be the left wing's job to stay wide for a pass as the right wing moved into scoring position.

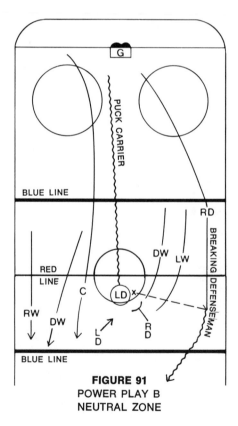

FIGURE 91
POWER PLAY B
NEUTRAL ZONE

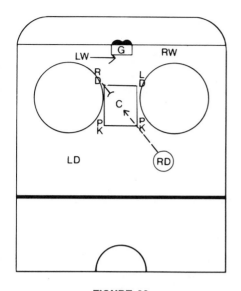

FIGURE 92
POWER PLAY
ATTACKING ZONE

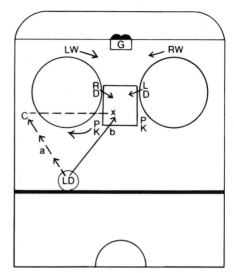

FIGURE 93
POWER PLAY
ATTACKING ZONE RETURN PASS

The give-and-go in the attacking zone, as shown in figure 93, can be developed in many ways. In this instance, the center has swung wide on the same side of the rink as the puck. The center is looking for a pass that will draw the penalty killer toward him. When he gets it, he'll give the left defenseman, who should automatically break for the net, a quick return pass. The ability to move quickly is very important when you are trying to force a mistake.

The center has other options if the penalty killer doesn't move at him to allow the return pass to the defenseman (figure 94). He can take a quick look for an open man. He should find the left wing wide, because the puck is on the left side of the ice. The center can probably set up a give-and-go with his left wing. He should drop a pass into the corner to the left wing and break for the net, looking for a return pass.

There are some teams that like to move the puck around the outside of the defenders' box and wait for a defensive breakdown that will enable them to slide a pass to the center who is parked in front of the net. In figure 95 the right wing has possession of the puck

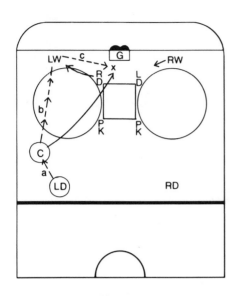

FIGURE 94
POWER PLAY
ATTACKING ZONE

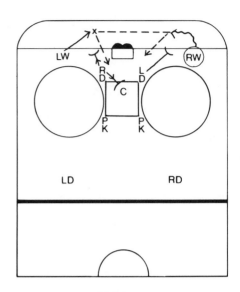

FIGURE 95
POWER PLAY
ATTACKING ZONE—SET UP CENTER

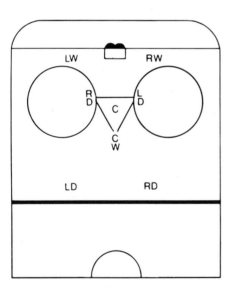

FIGURE 96
POWER PLAY
FIVE-ON-THREE

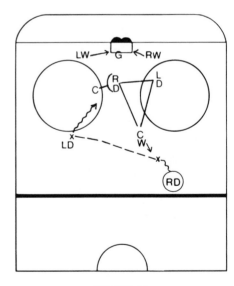

FIGURE 97
POWER PLAY
FIVE-ON-THREE—CENTER SCREEN

deep in the corner. He'll try to beat the left defenseman by drawing him out of position and centering pass to his teammate in the slot. If that situation doesn't develop, another option is for the left wing to move behind the net to take a pass and then to see if he can force a mistake on his side of the ice that might allow him to put the puck on the stick of his center, in the slot.

When a five-on-three situation develops (figure 96), hold on to the puck. You should be able to keep possession until you can set up a teammate for a direct shot. Don't have a defenseman or anybody else winding up to take a big slapshot under these circumstances. Work the puck around with quick passing to find an open man.

In figure 97 the center can clear a path directly to the net by using his body to screen off the right defenseman, while letting his left defenseman skate right to the net. Notice how the two wings are always ready to move into position at the mouth of the goal to take a pass, deflect a shot, or collect a rebound.

You'll find that most teams will use a three-man triangle. Some clubs will always keep one penalty killer on the top of the triangle, with a defenseman back in the area of the net. Jack Kelley, the former coach of the New England Whalers and general manager, advocates rotating the three men so that the nearest man to the puck becomes the top point of the triangle. And under this system, the penalty killer could end up at a defenseman's corner and a defenseman could be at the top of the triangle. Obviously, it takes a little work.

Use your defensemen out on the points at the blue line in this five-on-three situation because it's very hard to cover a great deal of the ice with just three skaters. They should have time to survey the situation, and they should be able to make the good pass that will set up a scoring chance.

DEFENSIVE PLAY

When the opposition moves into your defensive zone, it is vital for everyone to know where he should be at all times. Some teams lose their discipline under pressure and start chasing the puck. This usually means that an attacker is left unattended and in position to receive a pass that could result in a goal.

There is more than one way to set up areas of responsibility in your defensive zone. I like the basic plan offered in figure 98. This particular system calls for the wings to cover the points, with the center as the free man helping in front of his net and being directly responsible for the opposing center or whichever attacking player winds up in the slot.

In this system, there should always be a defenseman covering in front of the net. If the puck is to the right of the goaltender, the right defenseman should be the man on the puck. The defenseman should play the body in this situation, either tying up the man with the puck or effectively using his own body to separate the puck from the puck carrier. Obviously, if the puck is in the corner to the left of the goaltender, it's the left defenseman's duty to play the puck.

The two defensemen must work together and get to know each other's moves. There will be times when an adjustment will have to be made because the left defenseman ends up on the right side. It's easy enough for the right defenseman to realize when this is happening, and he should quickly move in front of the net to cover that area.

A quick word of warning for the defenseman who ends up covering the attacking forward in front of the net (figure 99). Know where the puck is and know where the opponent is. Don't get lured out of position while creeping over to try to pick up the puck, unless you are certain you will gain possession of the puck. Concentrate on covering the man in front, and don't let him get behind you. Always be able to touch him with your stick, hand, or body so that he won't be able to get good scoring opportunity. The only time you are released from this job is if the puck carrier beats your teammate and skates from the corner to directly in front of the net. You have to make a decision in this instance. Is he going to walk out and score, or is he trying to draw you toward him to make.a centering pass? You have to block the centering pass, or you have to use your body and hit the man as he tries to make his way in front of the net.

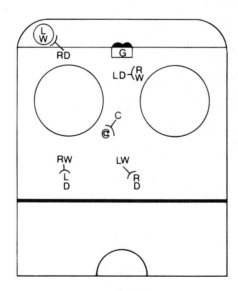

FIGURE 98
DEFENSIVE ZONE COVER
WINGS ON POINTS

FIGURE 99. The defenseman must know where the puck is and where the attacker is standing when protecting in front of the net.

A second system of covering in the defensive zone calls for the center to cover the points, with the two wings deep in the zone checking the opposition wings, as shown in figure 100. This allows one defenseman to concentrate on the puck, while the other defenseman takes up his station in front of the goaltender.

This system requires a strong-skating center, and the wings have to be more alert to help out, too. The wing on the opposite side of the ice from the puck should move into the slot area to help cover, as is shown in figure 100 by the positional play of the left wing. This insures good coverage in front of your goal and is particularly effective against a team that doesn't like to move the puck back to the points.

Forechecking is an important defensive tool even though it's used in the attacking zone. Your team should begin to think and play defense the instant you give up the puck—whether it's lost in the defensive zone, neutral zone, or attacking zone.

Generally, most teams will send one skater at the man with the puck, trying to force him to make a mistake. The quicker you move

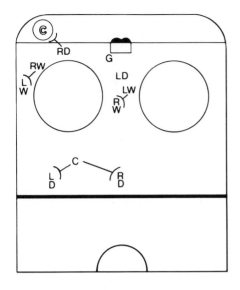

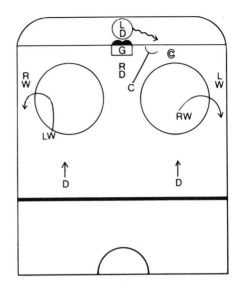

FIGURE 100
DEFENSIVE ZONE COVER
CENTER ON POINTS

FIGURE 101
FORECHECK—1 MAN

at the puck carrier, the better the chance that he'll rush a pass or find some way to give up possession. The center, as shown in figure 101, is usually the man to do the heavy forechecking in deep, while his two wings quickly turn toward the men they are supposed to cover—when backchecking with the opposing wings. But again, good team play would dictate that the first man in the zone, whoever he is, should go right to work forechecking, with the center moving over to pick up the wing's backchecking assignment, as shown in figure 102.

There are situations in which your team will want to move more than one forechecker in deep, forcing the play. This is usually done against defensemen who don't handle the puck well. It is also done when your team is down a goal or two and trying to force a mistake that could produce the goal that would put you back into the game. In figure 103, the left wing is "cheating" as he moves into the slot area to back up the forechecker and prevent the defenseman from head-maning the puck to the opposing center. A triangle should develop, as shown in figure 104, with the two wings ready to move

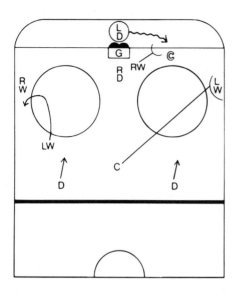

FIGURE 102
FORECHECK—1ST MAN (RW)

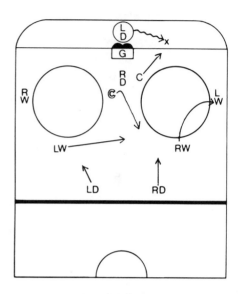

FIGURE 103
FORECHECK
WING BACKS UP CENTER

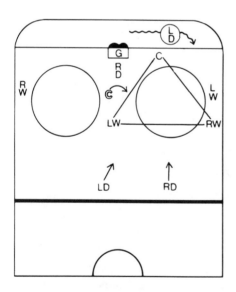

FIGURE 104
FORECHECK—PUCK IN CORNER

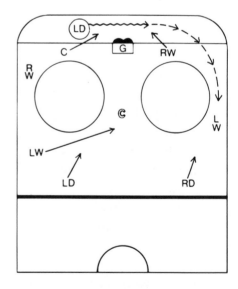

FIGURE 105
TWO-MAN PRESSURE FORECHECKING

into action if the first man in the zone doesn't stop the break-out play.

The real pressure should come from an all-out effort to play the man with the puck, as shown in figure 105. The center should move at the left defenseman and use his body to separate the puck carrier from the puck. At the same time, the right wing moves directly at the puck carrier, too. You'll notice that the right defenseman can move up to help cover the left wing, while the defensive left wing can move into the slot area to shut off the opposing center.

A team that skates well can always move at the man with the puck to put on heavy pressure. The center in figure 106 has made a move at the puck carrier, and the right wing should also jump in to apply more pressure, with hopes of coming up with the puck.

Notice that in this instance the left wing is again moving into the middle to help out. In fact, he'll be in perfect scoring position if the forechecker gains possession of the puck. Again, the defensemen have to use judgment and help out with these pressure tactics. Also notice how the center recovers to backcheck with the left wing.

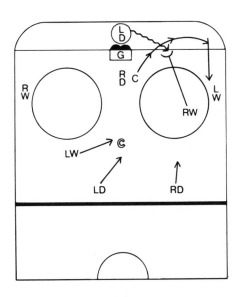

FIGURE 106
BACKUP FORECHECK

Play in the defensive zone should be controlled by the defensemen. They have to read the attack as it breaks up ice against them. It's good for a young hockey player to call out what's coming at him so that he and his defensive partner will be sure they are seeing the same thing. If it's a two-on-two, as shown in figure 107, you must be sure not to be confused by the crossover pattern of the attacking forwards. Be sure to shut off the middle to the puck carrier if he carries the puck in front of you and heads toward your defensive partner. Don't turn and give chase. It's your job to pick up the trailing wing.

When faced with a two-on-one, as shown in figure 108, jump up ice and try to force the puck carrier off the shooting angle. But the most important thing to remember is to stay between the two attackers. If you forget and drift in the direction of the puck carrier, you will leave the other wing wide open for a centering pass.

The three-on-two, as shown in figure 109, requires discipline. You'll notice that the wing carrying the puck is carrying it deep into the face-off circle, trying to bring the right defenseman with him.

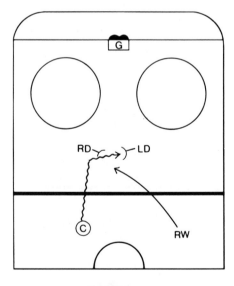

FIGURE 107
TWO-ON-TWO SWITCH

114

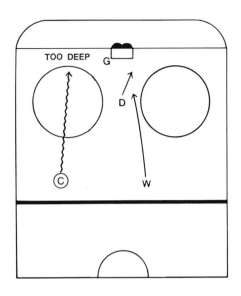

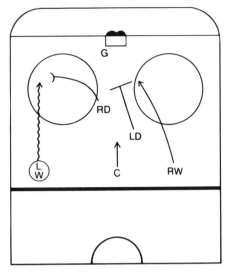

FIGURE 108
TWO-ON-ONE
FORCE SHOOTER OFF ANGLE

FIGURE 109
THREE-ON-TWO
NO BACKCHECKERS

But the right defenseman has successfully played him off the angle, and so the left defenseman is able to stand up in the middle, ready to cover the remaining attackers. He can move quickly at the center if the puck goes back into the slot, and he can shut off the traffic in front of the net if the pass is intended to go in that direction.

A hard-working backchecker is the defenseman's best friend when a three-on-two or a similar type of attack moves up the ice. If help is coming back, it usually allows the defenseman to stay up at the blue line and force the play. The defenseman should tell the backchecker who he should pick up as the play develops. Backcheckers shouldn't chase after the puck carrier. This is the defensemen's job. Generally a backchecker's job is to pick up the wide wing. In some instances, as shown in figure 110, the backchecker will have to pick up the trailer. The left wing has carried the puck into the face-off circle, and the right defenseman has moved over to play him in a man-to-man situation because his defensive partner has the right wing covered and the backchecker has the center covered in the slot area.

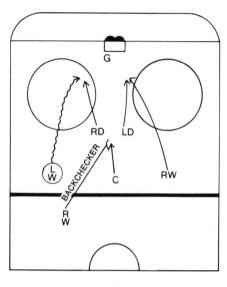

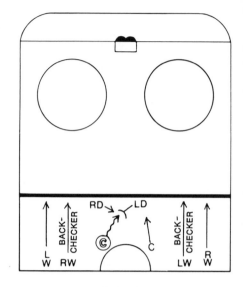

FIGURE 110
THREE-ON-TWO
ONE BACKCHECKER

FIGURE 111
THREE-ON-TWO
TWO BACKCHECKERS

If there are two backcheckers working with a three-on-two jump up ice, as shown in figure 111, then the defensemen must stand right up to the puck carrier and try to make a play in the neutral zone. When the center carries the puck over the red line, the left defenseman moves at him, ready to separate him from the puck with a solid body check or a poke check, depending on what he feels the situation calls for. The left defenseman has little to worry about with this type of support. The right defenseman is behind him, backing up his effort, while the backcheckers are moving stride for stride with the attacking wings.

A special style must be developed for forechecking when your team is shorthanded. The penalty killers must get to know each others' moves. If the first man in moves at the puck carrier, as shown in figure 112, the other checking wing must swing away from the play and pick up an open wing. The first man in must stop on the spot and start backchecking, being sure to skate after the remaining wing if the play moves past him. If this is done properly, the backcheck-

116

ers will arrive in the defensive zone ready to form the box needed to kill the penalty.

Teams that don't have exceptionally strong forecheckers will often let the other team break out of their own end without harassment, preferring instead to have each wing pick up a wing as the play moves up the ice, as shown in figure 113.

There are times when you are shorthanded but the situation late in the game demands that you try to make a break for your team. In cases such as this, the first man in can quickly forecheck, with the other forechecker backing up the play by trying to steal the puck. This strategy is dangerous because a good clearing pass will catch both penalty killers deep and will give the opposition a jump into the attacking zone. Nevertheless, late in the game it becomes a necessary tactic.

Another variation would have the penalty killers picking up wings and the defenseman moving in quickly to try to force a mistake, as shown in figure 114.

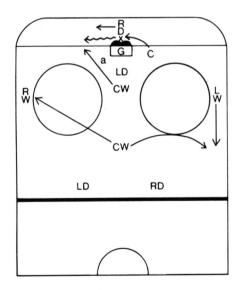

FIGURE 112
SHORTHANDED FORECHECK 1

a—forces play and picks up open winger.

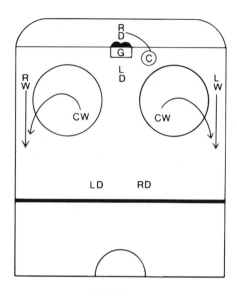

FIGURE 113
SHORTHANDED FORECHECK 2

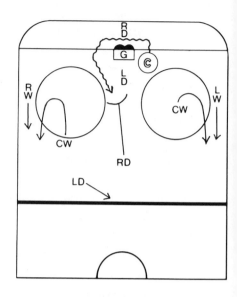

FIGURE 114
SHORTHANDED FORECHECK 3

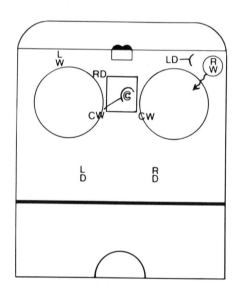

FIGURE 115
SHORTHANDED DEFENSIVE END

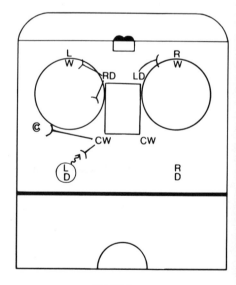

FIGURE 116
SHORTHANDED DEFENSIVE END

Once the play moves into your defensive end of the ice, the short-handed team must set up a box and try to keep the puck on the outside of the box. You'll notice in figure 115 that the left defenseman has moved at the right wing who has possession in the corner. The key man here is the penalty killer at the far corner of the box. He must be alert and move into the slot to cover the center. If the right wing slides the puck back to the right point, the left defenseman should quickly return to his corner on the box as should the penalty killer who was forced to move into the slot.

The penalty killers must develop a lot of patience. They should avoid chasing the puck and getting caught out of position. They must be quick to read situations and respond to them. In figure 116, the penalty killer has to cover two men at the top of the box. He must not rush at the left defenseman who has the puck and risk leaving the center unguarded. He has to be aware of both players. The right defenseman also has to be alert. He must protect against the left wing moving into the slot, but he must also be ready to check the center if the left defenseman is able to spring his center free.

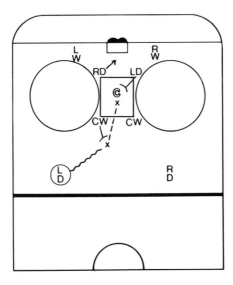

FIGURE 117
SHORTHANDED DEFENSEMAN SAGS

Even when shorthanded, the defensemen should work together to be sure someone is covering in front of the net. If the left defenseman makes a play at the center in the slot, as shown in figure 117, the right defenseman should sag off the left wing and begin to think about what may be going to happen in front of his net.

There aren't many variations for playing five-against-three. A triangle has to be set up, with the penalty killer at the top trying to cover both points as shown in figure 118. It's possible to rotate the triangle if the penalty-killing unit works together, as shown in figure 119. In our example, the left defenseman draws the penalty-killing wing toward him and then slides a pass along the ice to the right defenseman. The man capable of putting the most pressure on the right defenseman out on the blue line is the defensive team's left defenseman. He must move at the puck carrier, while the right defenseman moves over to play defense on the left side, and the wing drops back quickly to form the triangle as a defenseman.

There are many things to remember when you are out on the ice and the other team has possession of the puck. It's hard for begin-

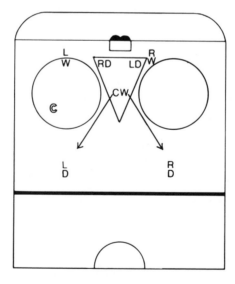

FIGURE 118
SHORTHANDED—TWO MEN

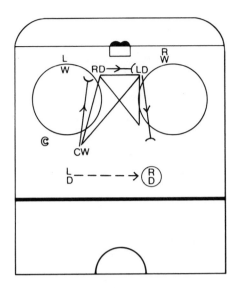

FIGURE 119
SHORTHANDED—TWO MEN (ROTATION)

ning players to think defensively when most of the glory goes to the goal scorers. But it's the two-way player who makes a team a winner.

A note of caution—don't be too quick to shift your gears to offense when a player on your team picks up the puck in your end. Be certain he has full possession and is ready to head-man the puck. Too often, a defender takes the puck away but gives it right back.

Always know each other's jobs in the defensive zone so that if the first man back into the defensive zone has to play out of position, somebody else will cover his territory.

GLOSSARY

ATTACKING ZONE   Area from an opponent's blue line to goal line where the goal cage is located.

BACKCHECKING   Skating back toward your own goal to help out defensemen and goaltender while trying to regain the puck from the opposition.

BEAT THE DEFENSE   To move past the defenseman and in on the goaltender.

BLIND PASS   Passing the puck without looking.

BOARDS   The enclosure of the playing surface.

BLUE LINE   The line at each end of the rink that defines the attacking zone. These lines are also used to determine off-sides. No attacking player may precede the puck over the defensive team's blue line.

BODY CHECK   Using your body (hip or shoulder) to stop an opponent.

BREAKAWAY   Puck carrier skating in alone on goaltender with no opposing player between him and the net.

CHECKING   Defending against or guarding an opponent. Harassing an opposing skater with the aim of making him surrender the puck.

COVER   A defensive player covering an opponent closely in his own defensive end so that he can't receive a pass.

CREASE   The rectangular area marked off in front of each net.

CURVED STICK   A stick with a hook in the blade as opposed to a straight stick.

DEFENSIVE ZONE   Area from goal line to blue line where team's own goal cage is located.

DEKE   To fake a man out of position while carrying the puck.

DRAW   Another way of saying face-off.

DRIBBLE   To move the puck from side to side or back and forth with the blade of your stick.

DROP PASS   To leave the puck for a trailing teammate to pick up.

FACE-OFF   The dropping of the puck between two players to start or resume play.

FLIP PASS   To lift the puck softly over an opponent's stick while making a pass.

FLOATER   Offensive player who slips behind the attacking defenseman looking for a breakaway. Also called sleeper or hanger.

FORECHECKING   Checking an opponent in his defensive zone as he attempts to start a play.

FREEZING THE PUCK   Pinning the puck against the boards with either your skate or your stick to force a stoppage in play and a face-off.

HAT TRICK   Three or more goals by a single player in one game.

HEAD-MAN   A quick lead pass to a teammate breaking up ice.

HEAD-MANNING   Always advancing the puck to a teammate up ice.

HIP CHECK   To use your hip to knock an opponent offstride.

ICING THE PUCK   Shooting the puck from behind the center red line across an opponent's goal line when both teams are skating at equal strength.

MITE   Young players eight years of age or less.

NEUTRAL ZONE   The center ice area between the blue lines.

PEE-WEE   The age category for boys 11 and 12.

OFF-SIDE   A violation called when an attacking player precedes the puck across the opponent's blue line.

OFF-SIDE PASS   A violation called when the puck is passed to a teammate across two or more lines.

PASS-OUT   A centering pass from behind or from the sides of the net made by an attacking player to a teammate stationed in scoring position in front of the net; also, a clearing pass from your defensive zone to a teammate in the neutral zone.

PENALTY-KILLER   A player whose job it is to use up time while a teammate is serving a penalty. The best penalty killers are fast skaters who can break up a power play.

PLAYMAKER   The player who sets up various plays and gives direction. Most often this is the center.

POINTS   Defenseman's position on the attacking blue line.

POKE CHECK   To make a sudden jab at the puck with your stick.

POWER PLAY   The situation in which the team with a man advanage during the course of a penalty sends five men into the shorthanded team's defensive zone.

PUCK   The vulcanized rubber disk used in hockey.

PULLING THE GOALTENDER   Taking the goaltender off ice to replace him with a forward as an extra skater. This is a last-minute attempt to score a goal when a team is behind and the game is almost over.

REBOUND   A shot that bounces off the goaltender or his equipment.

RED LINE   The line that divides the ice surface in half.

RUSH   The situation in which a player or his team carries the puck into the opponent's defensive zone.

SAVE   Stop made by the goaltender.

SCRAMBLE   Players battling for the puck in close-range action.

SCREEN SHOT   A shot through a group of players the goaltender is unable to see because of the men between himself and the shooter.

SHORTHANDED   A team with a man in the penalty box that is skating one less man during the course of action.

SLAP SHOT   A shot in which the player winds up and slaps his stick at the puck.

SLOT   The area directly in front of the net.

SPLITTING THE DEFENSE   A puck carrier breaking through two defensemen.

SQUIRT   Young players nine and 10 years of age.

STICK LIE   The angle between the blade and the shaft of the stick.

STICKHANDLING   The art of carrying the puck with the stick.

SWEEP CHECK   A sweeping motion, with stick flat on ice, that allows you to hook the puck away from an opponent.

TRAILER   Player who follows his teammates, giving the impression that he is out of play, but then moves into position to take a drop pass.

UNCOVERED   A player left unguarded in front of the net.

INDEX

Skating (*cont.*)
    Stride, 17–21
    Turning, 21
Stanley Cup, *v*
Stapleton, Pat, 67
Stick, 4, 8, 30, 70, 75
    Goaltender's stick, 10
    Handling of, 29–32, 34
    See Lie
Surface, skating, 1. *See* Rink

T

Tarasov, Anatoli, 83
Tremblay, J. C., 70

W

Wing, 1–2. *See* Positions
World Hockey Association
    (WHA), *vi*, 7

Y

Youth League, 15

Z

Zone, 1
    Defensive, 1
    Neutral, 1
    Offensive (attacking), 1